D0317432

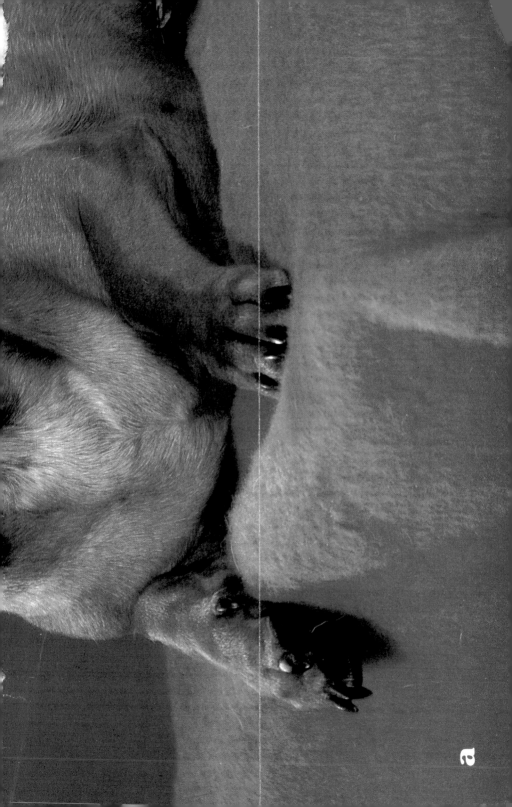

Dachshunds

HART

Edited by the Staff of T.F.H. Publications

Portions of this book (Origin and History, The Miniature Dachshund, Temperament and Personality, Exercise and Environment, Your New Dachshund Puppy, Grooming) originally appeared in *Dachshunds,* by Dorothy Allison Horswell and Laurence Alden Horswell. Other sections were compiled and edited by the staff of T.F.H. Publications. This new T.F.H. edition has been updated and enhanced with full-color photographs.

Distributed in the UNITED STATES by T.F.H. Publications, Inc., 211 West Sylvania Avenue, Neptune City, NJ 07753; in CANADA by H & L Pet Supplies Inc., 27 Kingston Crescent, Kitchener, Ontario N2B 2T6; Rolf C. Hagen Ltd., 3225 Sartelon Street, Montréal 382 Quebec; in ENGLAND by T.F.H. Publications Limited, 4 Kier Park, Ascot, Berkshire SL5 7DS; in AUSTRALIA AND THE SOUTH PACIFIC by T.F.H. (Australia) Pty. Ltd., Box 149, Brookvale 2100 N.S.W., Australia; in NEW ZEALAND by Ross Haines & Son, Ltd., 18 Monmouth Street, Grey Lynn, Auckland 2 New Zealand; in SINGAPORE AND MALAYSIA by MPH Distributors (S) Pte., Ltd., 601 Sims Drive, # 03/07/21, Singapore 1438; in the PHILIPPINES by Bio-Research, 5 Lippay Street, San Lorenzo Village, Makati Rizal; in SOUTH AFRICA by Multipet Pty. Ltd., 30 Turners Avenue, Durban 4001. Published by T.F.H. Publications Inc., Ltd. the British Crown Colony of Hong Kong.

Contents

Poster A: A trained Dachshund is a good subject for photography. Robert Pearcy has captured the desirable features of the head and front of this smooth haired red Dachshund.

Poster B: It is quite safe to allow your Dachshund to settle on top of your furniture. It is a breed without a strong doggy odor.

Poster C: Breeders of Dachshund, as well as other breeds, strive to produce litters of identical puppies. Uneven progeny means lack of genetic purity in the parents chosen.

Introduction

The proper introduction to a book like this one is a list of other good ones about dogs, because no relatively small book could hope to cover comprehensively all of the specialized topics that a serious dog fancier can become involved with. Breeding, training, exhibiting, health care—they're all important topics, each one deserving a big volume of its own for proper exposition. The following books are all published by T.F.H. Publications and are recommended to you for additional information.

Dog Behavior, Why Dogs Do What They Do by Dr. Ian Dunbar (H-1016) is a thorough and enlightening exploration of all aspects of canine behavior and the relationship between man and dog. The author, a noted specialist in the field of animal behavior, discusses canine communication, social and sexual behaviors, and the physical and sensory capacities and capabilities of dogs, among other topics.

Dog Training by Lew Burke (H-962) reveals the secrets behind the methods successfully used by the author, a premier trainer of dogs for individuals, industry, and the government. Lew Burke concentrates on understanding dogs' needs in relation to the needs of their owner, and he uses dogs' psychological makeup to keep dogs happy by being obedient.

Successful Dog Show Exhibiting by Anna Katherine Nicholas (H-993) is an excellent how-to manual for purebred dog owners who are thinking about entering the world of dog show competition. The book includes detailed explanations of dog show classes, step-by-step descriptions of the judging process (including what the judge looks for), ring behavior do's and don'ts for both dog and handler, and advantages and disadvantages of professional handlers versus showing your own dog. The author, a judge who's been part of the world of dogs for over 50 years, knows her subject well and makes it understandable for the reader.

Dog Owner's Encyclopedia of Veterinary Medicine by Allan H. Hart, B.V.Sc. (H-934) is a comprehensive treatise on canine disease and disorders. It is written on the premise that dog owners should recognize the symptoms and understand the treatments of most diseases of dogs, so that dog owners can properly communicate with their veterinarian or give treatment to their dogs. Proper nutrition, parasite problems, and first-aid measures are also described.

Origin and History

Dachshund is pronounced dox-hoont (oo as in foot). In German, *Dachs* means badger; *Hund* means dog; *Dachshund* thus means "badger dog" in the same way we say "bird dog" or "rabbit dog." Affectionate German diminutives include "Dackel" and "Teckel."

Few breeds escape from partisan rivalry dating back to remote antiquity—although all breeds share the same derivation from common prehistoric canine prototypes—with no valid evidence tracing any continuity from far-fetched forebears, fostered by folklore or fantasy. Claims of Egyptian origin for Dachshunds, based on carvings (from about 1500 B.C.) of short-legged dogs (one with a hieroglyphic name translated as "Tekal") ignore the fact that there were no badgers in Egypt—so no "badger" dog. Nor do they trace linguistic or biological connections with a dog developed to hunt badgers and so named in Germany at least 3,000 years and 1,000 dog generations later. Daniel's interpretation of the Old Testament handwriting on the wall (*Mene, Mene, Tekel, Upharsin*) defines Tekel as "weighed in the balances and found wanting"—an apt epitaph on illusory ancient origin!

Earliest records now available of *dogs* hunting *badgers* include several woodcuts in a book first published in 1560. These dogs had long bodies, short legs, medium-length heads, pendent ears, short necks, and sickle tails. It is noteworthy that there are smooth coats and suggestions of longhaired coats in the longer furnishings on ears, culottes, and tails of some of the dogs illustrated. The name "Dachshund" has been traced back to a book in German and Latin in 1681, and there are paintings dating from 1735 of unmistakable Dachshunds, identified by name as such.

German history—The real origin of the Dachshund breed is embraced in the 300 years (1550-1850) during which the German forester-gamekeepers and sportsmen among the land-owning gentry—at first selecting dogs for their success in hunting badgers underground—gradually produced a "badger dog" better adapted by structure and temperament to cope with the dangerous claws and fangs of this formidable 25- to 40-pound antagonist. Girth of chest determines the size of burrow a Dachshund can penetrate and, therefore, the size of the adversary in residence. Always facing the possibility of a death struggle underground, where no human help

Origin and History

could avail, a Dachshund's self-reliant use of its own armament of jaws and teeth must settle the question of survival. A Dachshund head and neck, inadequate to balance its body, would be no match for the defending opponent, any more than any small-caliber weapon is effective against large-caliber game. Within depth and height limits of the bore of the average badger tunnel, successive Dachshund generations converged more and more toward a pattern balancing punishing head with length of neck and body and "retractable" running gear, and combining maximum combat capacity with maximum maneuverability. Male and female Dachshunds were used interchangeably for hunting—there was no distinction of warrior armed for battle and delicately proportioned chatelaine pursuing cultural arts at home. In addition, left to her own devices, a mother Dachshund would be responsible for bringing home the game to feed her litter. Among Dachshunds, there is no excuse for a "weaker sex," no feminine discount for head and neck equally needed for defense and offense by both sexes.

There were many other forms of game in German forests besides badgers; and because of their versatility, Dachshunds were encouraged to seek out small game on the surface and, on a five-meter leash to trail wounded game including large deer, to dispatch them and recover the venison. In packs, they also were employed successfully against wild boar. However, as their name emphasizes, their structure was specialized for pursuing appropriate game underground. By the time of the earliest preserved breeding records—about a century ago—Dachshund type, as we distinguish it today from other breeds, had become clearly defined and stabilized. Since then, this type has been continuously improved, and the ratio of good Dachshunds has been constantly increased by selective breeding.

American history—Earliest American records show Dachshunds first imported to the United States between 1879 and 1885; eleven Dachshunds appear in Volume II of the Stud Book of the American Kennel Club, published the latter year. Most imports have come from Germany, the country of origin; others have come from Austria, Holland, Sweden, and England.

Until after World War I, most of the comparatively few Dachshunds in this country belonged to people

Origin and History

from Germany or with German contacts. During that war, Dachshunds—considering their built-in resistance to regimentation —were very unfairly used as cartoon symbols to rally anti-German sentiment, and the breed received a severe setback. A very long time ago, when we walked our Dachshunds every day in New York City, we were challenged by unfriendly comments of "Frankfurter dogs" and "German sausage dogs." To admire Dachshunds was regarded as much of an acquired taste as smoked oysters or Greek olives.

The Dachshund Club of America carried on a successful "educational" public relations campaign during World War II, particularly directed to newspaper and magazine editors and cartoonists, reminding them that most of the human population of this country is descended from "imported" ancestry; that the few imported Dachshunds have been "naturalized" by re-registration with the A.K.C. (American Kennel Club); that Dachshunds born here— never less than ninety-nine percent of the breed—are as much entitled to be considered American as any other American-born population. The standing of the breed, as

reflected in registrations and in dog-show participation, was well sustained through these hostilities, and now Dachshunds are accepted as completely as any breed.

Functional design—Badger earths were not air-conditioned. As oxygen was reduced by repeated breathing, it became necessary to breathe a larger volume of the depleted air to support maximum exertion. Lungs extend back as far as the soft ribs, which help the diaphragm act as bellows; the oval cross-section of the chest provides liberal room for lungs and heart without extending the shoulder structure to excessive width. The longer the rib-cage, the more air could be processed, and a long rib-cage also helps support the long back, resembling in design box girders.

To move this long body freely through badger burrows, it was necessary for the legs to fold to a minimum length. Anyone experimenting with a carpenter's rule can convince himself that three sections of equal length can fold shorter and extend longer than any comparable sections of unequal lengths. In the forequarters, the shoulder blade, upper arm, and forearm (elbow to wrist) do this folding. In the hindquarters, the

Origin and History

thigh and shin bones and the "bone" from hock joint to foot are so folded in crawling through a burrow or under a bureau. Fully extended at a gallop, these same short Dachshund legs can cover an unexpected amount of ground.

When wild animals digging their tunnels encountered a rock or a large root, they dug around or over it, leaving a constriction. If an eager Dachshund forced its chest past such an obstruction and had to back up to get clear, it became important that the breastbone of the after chest have the same gradual sled-runner up-curve as the forechest, like a shoehorn, to ease the chest over the obstruction in either direction. A cut-up (chicken-breasted) after-chest could be "hung" over such an obstacle as though by an anchor fluke. A properly constructed Dachshund, with forelegs at the deepest point of the hammock-shaped keel, can crawl through a tunnel which just clears its depth from keel to withers, equally able to move its legs ahead or back. Turned-out "digging" front feet (once said to "throw dirt to the sides" where there is no room for it in a tunnel) have been replaced by snug arched feet with forward alignment. Too heavy a chest or too coarse bone are as much of a

handicap as underdevelopment. A properly proportioned Dachshund suggests the symmetrical build and lithe agility of the middle-weight boxing champion.

A long head provides suitable accommodation for keen scenting ability and for strong jaws and teeth of maximum effectiveness, with scissor fit of incisors, interlocking fangs, and shearing capacity of molars. Eyes are protected by a deep setting and a well-developed surrounding bone structure. Ears set on high and well back can be drawn up over the neck out of harm's way, like small braided pigtails. A neck of good length serves the thrusting and parrying purposes of a fencer's nimble wrist. Even a tail of good size and length, in continuation of the spine, has been used by a hunter's long arm forcibly to rescue many a Dachshund from places of great tightness.

A Dachshund whose skin was elastic enough to stretch and slip like a loose glove had an advantage for working in constricted space. But as soon as released, the skin should snap back to a slick fit, like the modern two-way-stretch foundation garment, for a wrinkle of loose skin, by folding over, could (like a clutch) grip a dog in tight quarters. Loose skin around head

Origin and History

The legs of a Dachshund are short but when moving swiftly are capable of propelling the dog over a wide area in a short time.

and throat could be grasped or torn by an adversary, resulting in dangerous loss of blood; skin hanging around the ankles, like wrinkled socks, also is undesirable.

To avoid fatigue, straight legs with parallel gait like locomotive side-rods make efficient use of muscular energy. Viewed from the side, front- and hind-leg action suggesting a broad capital "A" expends this energy on desirable reach and thrust, walking or trotting with surprising, apparently effortless speed and split-second rocket-like "low-gear" getaway. The ninety-degree upper-arm to shoulder-blade angulation (each forty-five degrees from the vertical) provides "shock-absorber" action, running or jumping. A fair clearance under the breastbone is needed, as under an automobile crankcase, to clear rough ground or the treads of a staircase. Pawing the air, like the goosestep, under chin or belly, or throwing feet in or out waste energy and are undesirable. So are "dancing" or "weaving" gaits, short stilted steps, or too many other variations from the correct gait. The back should stay level in motion; it should not roach, sag, or bounce.

Coats and sizes—Two kinds of coats were developed early: the *smooth* and the *longhaired*. During the nineteenth century, to protect from briar and bramble, a third variety, with a harsh, wiry, terrier-type coat, with water-repellent undercoat, was developed—the *wirehaired*. The badger-hunting weight of thirty to forty pounds was reduced for fox to sixteen to twenty pounds; and since the turn of the twentieth century, for smaller vermin and cottontail rabbits, *miniature Dachshunds* of all three coats have been bred down as small as six and five pounds and are increasing in popularity as pets.

Origin and History

Colors—The original color of the Dachshund was brown, now officially called "red." However, when a hunter with a shotgun was nervously waiting for a quick brown fox to jump out of a burrow, chased by an equally quick and equally brown Dachshund, and the Dachshund beat the fox to the exit, you can guess what sometimes shouldn't have happened to the Dachshund! So, black-and-tan Dachshunds were developed by crossing to a small Bloodhound of that color, and occasional albino variants (dapples) have been highly prized as particularly suitable for trigger-happy hunters. Other albino variants with tan markings include chocolate and a mousy gray (called "blue").

Intangibles—Two intangible products of the formative centuries of the Dachshund also endure: the Dachshund bark, able to penetrate from burrow depths to the surface, and a uniquely self-reliant character developed in this one sporting breed, to engage its quarry in pursuit or mortal combat remotely underground, without guidance or support of a hunter. Dachshunds unable to rely upon themselves in the dark depths of the earth to come up with answers that worked just didn't come up at all to perpetuate

their indecisions. Small wonder that today they don't turn to people for much advice.

All in all, the Dachshunds that shared the foresters' working hours and activities also shared their homes and many of their relaxations. Their unusual proportions lent them to a whole miscellany of sympathetically humorous illustrations and anecdotes—relating the Dachshund to the enjoyment of beer, sausages, soft living, and convivial song—in which the native shrewdness of the Dachshund usually achieved its individualistic objectives. These attributes have become so much more widely known than their specialized hunting functions that outside of the German forests they more nearly represent the basis of the almost-universal appeal of the Dachshunds today.

It is unlikely that you ever will want your Dachshund pet to hunt underground. But the powerful, smooth lines of the underslung Dachshund chassis represent the evolution of a design just as functional as the most modern streamlined sports cars. Your understanding of how and why the Dachshund "got that way" will better enable you to appreciate its dynamic, elegant appearance.

The Miniature Dachshund

Miniature Dachshunds are not under-sized or undeveloped specimens of full-sized Dachshunds but were purposely produced to work in burrows smaller than standard-sized Dachshunds can enter. The limits set upon their weight and chest circumference resulted in more slender body structure. Depth of chest and shortness of leg proportionate to standard conformation would, in these diminutive animals, prove impractical. "Within the American size limit of 'under nine pounds at twelve months or older,' symmetrical adherence to the general Dachshund conformation, combined with smallness, and mental and physical vitality, should be the outstanding characteristics of miniature Dachshunds." Written in 1935, describing the ideal miniature, these are the operative words for the application of the American standard to American miniature Dachshunds.

Kaninchenhund—In the 1890's an attempt was made in Germany to quickly produce a dog with a chest-girth under ten inches, small enough to dash freely through their acres of rabbit warrens—like multiple public-housing for rabbits, inverted underground—to scare out the living prospective material for hassenpfeffer. Toy breeds used to shortcut the size-reduction also handed along toy temperament. These crash-dive, small-sized crossbred dogs would not hunt rabbits. The Kaninchenhund (rabbit dog) project collapsed, leaving behind a few spindling mixed-breed pets, some of whom resembled Dachshunds.

Zwerg and Kaninchenteckel—But rabbits still abounded, there in mother earth, like fish in the sea, free for the harvesting, so another approach was made—this time by experienced Dachshund breeders—to breed down in size from existing strains of *gebrauchs* teckel (working, *i.e.,* hunting Dachshunds) weighing around twelve pounds; this time, however, every individual retained in the size-reduction program was tested for "hunting passion" and any which did not prove true to type in this respect was discarded. By 1903, records disclose elaborate weight and chest circumference specifications (since World War II, German specifications no longer include weights, only chest-girth limits) and registrations of Zwerg (dwarf) teckel, and by 1918 of Kaninchen (rabbit) teckel, with chest girth limits to enable these breeds to scurry freely through cottontail burrows. (A *Dachs*hund

The Miniature Dachshund

hunts badgers, a *kaninchen*teckel hunts rabbits, but a *zwerg*teckel does not hunt dwarfs—although some have been trained to detect truffles! In Germany, puppies of Kaninchen sires and Zwerg dams are not classified until they are one year old. The slightly larger Zwergteckel incline toward better bone, substance, and type, more as sought in American Miniature Dachshund breeding.)

This utilitarian size-reduction program sacrificed Dachshund appearance to functional qualities of ferret-slim body and zeal to hunt rabbits. Whatever abnormal glandular or other metabolic factors contributed to rapid size-reduction also evoked torsionally-everted elbows and/or forefeet, leggy proportions, prominent round eyes, smaller muzzles, abrupt stops, domed skulls, and button ears—among the oldest breed faults, proving small size no mutation. None of these faults handicap speed through rabbit holes, and they were anchored by impatient close breeding, in ever-smaller males—however little some of the smallest "nasturtium seed" studs resembled acceptable Dachshunds. Because females carry and deliver puppies, they were spared extreme concentration of size reduction, and

they better maintained their conformation. There seems probably some sex-linkage with conformation, for to this day female miniatures more frequently develop creditable conformation than their litter-brothers. Few of the early German miniatures were exhibited at dog shows; many conformation judges refused to "rate" them or judge them. Their field trials were scored by how many rabbits each contestant was able to bolt in ten minutes by stop watch.

"Miniatures"—Zwerg and Kaninchenteckel were imported to this country in the early 1930's as "cute" canine novelties. The name "miniature" Dachshund was adopted in place of the more complicated German nomenclature, or the American "toy"; the complex German specifications were rounded off simply to "under nine pounds"; and a combined-coat-and-sex class was offered for them at the May 6, 1934 Hotel Pennsylvania specialty show of the Dachshund Club of America with nine entries by four owners. That autumn, several six-or seven-month puppies of standard parents won over miniature Dachshunds in this "under-nine-pound" class. To prevent such "ringers" from taking unfair advantage of this class, the

The Miniature Dachshund

minimum age of twelve months was added to the class definition in 1935, and the Miniature Class was made a division of the Open Class making blue-ribbon winners eligible to compete in Winners Classes with standard Dachshunds for championship points.

Early Americana—In this country, it is doubtful if one Dachshund in a thousand is used to hunt game. Here, the distinctive appeal of miniature Dachshunds as pets is diminutive and nimble, but well-balanced, unmistakable . Dachshund type. In this scaling-down process, clearance under the keel—already too low in many standard Dachshunds—cannot be reduced in proportion to other dimensions without curtailing their capacity to climb stairs, enter automobiles, or jump into your lap if invited.

Our first miniature won the first weight-and-age Miniature Class at Westminster in 1935 and enough more that first year for the first "phantom" miniature championship. Her eight-pound size, good looks, and beguiling disposition helped favorably to introduce miniature Dachshunds in the East and Midwest. Another miniature that matured at four-and-a-quarter pounds, while less symmetrical in

conformation, could go almost anywhere in a jacket pocket; she learned to relax under a napkin in restaurants where no one suspected her presence until she followed us out the door when we left. A six-pound miniature we took along on a rail and plane trip to California was permitted (in a shoulder-holster pouch) to sit at the dining-car table for dinner, and the Pullman conductor beamed while she held court in the observation car. Hotels asked questions only if her crate appeared in the lobby. On only one of five planes we used did regulations require us to be separated.

Early problems—In the first decade of miniature breeding in America, there were so few miniatures, either imported from Germany or their immediate descendants—using the German gauge of three generations of unmixed miniature ancestry—that sound breeding plans were difficult to develop and harder still to carry out. All miniature stock had comparatively recent ancestors of standard size *and* ancestors in which faults linked with too-rapid size-reduction were concentrated. Whenever fairly close line-breeding was attempted to expedite a program, either improved quality

The Miniature Dachshund

brought with it increased size or reduced size entailed the same faults as in Germany: fiddle fronts, weedy structure, pop eyes, snipy muzzles, steep stops, apple domes, and bat ears.

A.K.C. position—These faults are among the reasons for the unwillingness of the A.K.C. to approve separate "variety" status for miniature Dachshunds; no breed variety is based upon weight limitation, weights having been manipulated by starvation and dehydration, neither practice to be encouraged. There is not enough difference in height at shoulder to separate miniatures from standard Dachshunds. Miniature breeding is not yet self-sustaining within their own size range. Separate miniature Winners Classes would entail complete miniature classification including Puppy Classes subject to the same objections as over twenty years ago. And with three coat varieties already established, separate varieties for the miniature size would complicate the classification by having an unprecedented result—six championship varieties in one breed.

Another problem has been that some exhibitors with animals they know to be of such structural size that in show condition they weigh more than nine pounds have imposed with too much success on misplaced "sportsmanship" of competitors and on reluctance or lethargy of judges and show officials toward weighing of miniatures to verify their eligibility to compete under nine pounds "on the day." In some parts of the country it is doubtful if miniature entries ever have been weighed. Some long-haired "miniatures" imported from England where they permit "miniature" weights up to eleven pounds, have been shown in America on comparatively remote show circuits where records indicate that they brought their own competition and were never weighed. Several wirehairs also have been shown to championship unweighed in the classes and then offered at stud as miniatures, well over nine pounds in show condition. Miniatures are being advertised at stud as weighing no more than seven pounds but have recently been weighed out of miniature classes as heavier than nine pounds.

Weighing—A.K.C. rules require that accurate scales be available at dog shows. In a weight-limited class, any officiating judge, or exhibitor in the ring by applying to the judge, has the right to insist that each miniature be weighed officially;

Temperament and Personality

accurate weights of all to be forwarded through superintendents or show secretaries to the A.K.C. as part of the show report; any found overweight to be so reported to the judge, to be so noted and disqualified in the judge's book. Assembling such accurate weights of as many miniatures as possible in competition will contribute constructively to the progress of miniatures.

Post-war improvement—In spite of these handicaps, gradually increasing numbers of loyal devotees of miniature Dachshunds persisted in breeding and exhibiting them; and in the many years since World War II, they have enjoyed a renaissance of interest and favor. Patience and perseverance with slower, more selective approaches to producing miniatures in the image of good Dachshunds—ever reinforced and intensified by exactions of competition with standard Dachshunds—have achieved the double goal of a number of individuals of real championship quality in all three coats, accomplished well under the original nine-pound weight limit. The next objective is to engender a broader average of such high quality more dependably among more miniature Dachshunds.

Dachshund disposition—For centuries, Dachshunds have lived harmoniously with people. A Dachshund can share every family mood, exuberant when you are gay, rarin' to go when you are ready for a walk, a ride, or a boisterous game; happy to curl up near you when you are engaged in a settled occupation (as this typing), and most responsive to every demonstration of your affection. It is a fallacy that all individuals of any one breed have this or that disposition. Temperaments vary; we have had Dachshunds "little pals of all the world," or preferring our family, sometimes one individual. We often can relate these choices to early environment. Each puppy inherits some degree of confident or shy temperament, and early associations often have lasting influences. Given a sound base, your regime can mold the finished product if you are firm, patient, and consistent.

Not to run free—However, self-reliant character is just as deeply rooted in the Dachshund as its two-dogs-long-and-half-a-dog-high proportions, and it introduces a most serious problem! No family should acquire a Dachshund that expects it to run loose; it is never safe from the hazards of street or

Temperament and Personality

highway traffic. Let a Dachshund be inspired to cross the street, and no consideration of approaching automobiles will enter its head.

Part of the price of enjoying a Dachshund through the engaging humorous months of its unfolding puppyhood, through the long vigorous plateau of its adult life, into the mellow late years, is never —repeat *never*—to turn a Dachshund loose where it has access to traffic or traffic has access to it.

Or be left alone—A dog is a gregarious animal. If your plan for living is such that a pet animal will be left alone as a daily regime, we recommend some other type of pet, although a *person* alone much of the time will find a world of comfort in a Dachshund's companionship. Don't make the mistake that one puppy provides good company for another puppy. Two puppies only become rivals for your attention—or they may revert to a canine community of their own, remote from people—and immensely complicate housebreaking and training. On the other hand, a Dachshund in its declining years may be stimulated by the presence of a puppy and, by its good example, can be of inestimable help in inducting a young successor to the ways of your household.

Captions for color photos on pages 17 through 24:
Page 17: Note the strongly developed legs of Dachshunds. Page 18: Like any other long-haired breed of dog, a longhaired Dachshund will require regular brushing and grooming. Photo courtesy of Kosmos Verlag. Page 19: Watch closely the diet of your Dachshund. Spinal problems are common in this breed on account of overeating. Photo by Vince Serbin. Pages 20-21: One can conveniently keep more than one Dachshund in a small house or city apartment. Page 22: A longhaired Dachshund puppy. Page 23: The most common two-colored Dachshund is the black and tan. Page 24: In spite of its short legs, ideally a Dachshund must move without dragging the body, not waddle like a duck, or turn the toes inward or outward. Photo by Robert Pearcy.

Captions for color photos on pages 57 through 64:
Page 57: An example of a show Dachshund. Photo by Sally Anne Thompson. Page 58: A Dachshund is just perfect sitting on one's lap. Page 59: A longhaired, one-colored Dachshund. At 12 months or over, a Miniature weighs not more than 9 pounds. Page 60: As seen here, the Dalmatian and the Dachshund are quite unlike in physical features. Page 61: After a bath, always dry off your Dachshund with a thick towel. Photo by Tom Caravaglia. Page 62: A trio of black and tan Dachshunds. Page 63: Regardless of hair type and color, a good Dachshund should have sufficiently dark eyes of medium size and oval shape. Page 64: These Dachshunds are obviously from the same litter.

Exercise and Environment

Cold or Hot—Even in zero weather, a Dachshund does not need a sweater or jacket outdoors, so long as it is exercising actively. If it is to stand around in frosty weather, cold wind, on wet ground, or ride in a drafty car, a garment is advisable. This may be any of several types of sweaters or coats. Be careful that it is not too tight. In *hot weather,* provide quarters that are shady, but not damp; keep fresh drinking water available, and limit exercise to the cooler early or late hours.

Exercise—After a puppy's frame is grown, from six months on, its muscular development depends upon the extent and nature of the exercise it gets. Each owner becomes a sculptor working constructively in the medium of living tissue. Steady consistent walking on leash builds up proper propulsion muscles in shoulders, back, and hindquarters to bring a Dachshund to its most perfect conformation. This appearance cannot be produced by irregular romping. Walking up to two miles a day also perfects a Dachshund's gait to most efficient application of muscular energy and maintains muscular condition.

Jumping—Jumping up or down should be discouraged or regulated. Dachshund proportions and structure were developed to function on or under the surface of the earth, not in the air. They should be trained to carry their weight on all four legs. *Jumping up* to heights greater than their own may over-develop hindquarters and cause the high croups which disfigure many Dachshund backlines. When *jumping down* from the height of a bed, or any but the lowest chairs—although the ninety-degree angulation of the shoulder-blade and upper-arm have shock-absorber design—the legs which constitute the landing gear are short for the weight and length of the body. Not only is there risk of strains or sprains of the joints involved, but also the whole shoulder assembly may be permanently sprung. There also is the hazard of spinal injury, which may result in some degree of posterior paralysis and take a long time for recovery, if at all. Such heights as ordinary steps are well within a Dachshund's capacity. None of ours has thought anything of briskly ascending or descending flights of straight or spiral stairs, which, after all, require only the repetition of a series of hops rather than jumps.

In automobiles do not let your Dachshund put its head out a window. Besides the risk that it may

Exercise and Environment

try to jump out, it is possible for something hard or sharp to damage an eyeball or for severe drafts to irritate ears. In hot weather, if the car stands in the sun, or where the sun may strike before you return, don't leave your Dachshund—it may be overcome by the heat. Even in certain shade, be sure that windows are opened at the top. The first time you take a puppy riding in a car, also take a newspaper, in case there is any car sickness. Until you are sure of its behavior, don't feed shortly before a car trip.

Fencing and caging—Partition the puppy's quarters from other rooms temporarily by using vertically sliding panels in doorways, in place of the folding lattice gates used for children. A piece of one-eighth-inch Masonite as wide as the doorway and about twenty-four inches high can be held in place by two strips of quarter-round fastened to the sides of the door frame by such thin brads that when ultimately removed, no scar will show. Such a panel can be lifted out at any time you want to remove it, can be stepped over by people, leaving the door "open" for their use. When a Dachshund cannot see through this opaque barrier, it won't be tempted to make a bad habit of standing up against it

and, thereby, over-develop its hindlegs to be taller than its shoulders or develop a concave backline. A fence, where a Dachshund makes a habit of standing up on its hindlegs, can have a horizontal opaque sheet-metal panel attached to the wire so that the Dachshund, standing on all four feet can see under the panel without crouching yet cannot see over it by standing up against it. For adults, make it from sixteen to thirty inches; for younger or smaller Dachshunds, start with the panel lower and move it up as needed. Sitting up on its haunches does a Dachshund no harm and is a good trick.

Crates especially designed for dogs will keep a puppy confined, when desired, to a small, safe space, movable around the house, in a car, or at a dog show. If occupied regularly, a fiber carton six inches deep, inside the crate, provides floor and draft-proof walls. In houses with areas not separated by walls or doors, a children's playpen with panelled sides makes a good "puppy area."

Your New Dachshund Puppy

Now, assuming that you have decided on a Dachshund and have decided the coat, color, and size you prefer, there remain the questions of which sex and what age.

Sex and Age—This is no place to undertake a "battle of the sexes!" Since no Dachshund should run loose, a female, during the brief sex-vulnerable intervals of estrum, twice a year, will be chaperoned whenever outdoors; or it is relatively easy to keep her safely confined or to board her with your veterinarian or at a reliable kennel. All her life she can alternate between indoor and outdoor bathroom facilities; she usually is more gently affectionate, particularly with young children. On the other hand, a male, after he reaches an age to lift his leg, must be let or taken outside to relieve himself four times every single day, no matter what the inconvenience. He may display embarrassing interest in the sex of other dogs he encounters; leave his "calling card" on every post, tree, shrub, or hydrant; and although housebroken at home, cannot always be trusted in unfamiliar private or public premises. We can't decide for you.

As to age, three months is young enough. By that age, a puppy is weaned and independent of its mother's care and company, day or night. It is well adapted to its diet and convenient meal schedule. It is old enough for vaccinations against distemper and other contagious diseases (in fact, a vaccination program may have already been started for the puppy by its seller) and is at the most responsive age to begin to understand and heed the lessons of housebreaking. A younger puppy requires frequent attention, approximating foster-mothering, which cannot be delegated to children or neglected even for a few hours. A lower price at a lower age is no bargain. After all this preparation, what remains to be done is so simple that you must not let it impress you as anticlimax, for nothing in this book is of more importance to the life-long enjoyment of the Dachshund you are about to bring into your family circle.

Selection—When you do pick out a Dachshund puppy as a pet, don't be hasty; the longer you study puppies, the better you will understand them. Make it your transcendent concern to select only one that radiates good health and spirit and is lively on its feet, whose eyes are bright, whose coat shines, and who comes forward eagerly to make and to cultivate your acquaintance. Don't fall for any shy

Your New Dachshund Puppy

little darling that wants to retreat to its bed or its box, or plays coy behind other puppies or people, or hides its head under your arm or jacket appealing to your protective instinct. Pick the puppy who forthrightly *picks you!* The feeling of attraction *should be mutual!*

Documents—Now, a little paper work—transfer of ownership and other papers which should accompany any puppy you buy, notes of immunization against puppy diseases, diet and feeding schedule to which the puppy is accustomed—and may we welcome you as a fellow owner to long pleasant association with a most lovable pet, a young Dachshund— and more (news) paper work.

Transportation—If you take the puppy home by car, protect it from drafts, particularly in cold weather. Wrapped in a towel and carried in the arms or lap of a passenger, it usually will make the trip without mishap. If it starts to drool and to squirm, stop the car for a few minutes. Have newspapers handy in case of car-sickness. A covered carton lined with newspapers provides protection for puppy and car, if you are driving alone. Avoid excitement and unneccessary handling of the puppy on arrival. It is a very small "package" to be

making a complete change of surroundings and company, and it needs frequent rest and refreshment to renew its vitality.

Playmates are another immediate problem if the new puppy is to be greeted by children or other pets. If not, you can skip this subject. The natural affinity between puppies and children calls for some supervision until a live-and-let-live relationship is established. This applies particularly to a Christmas puppy, when there is more excitement than usual and more chance for a puppy to swallow something upsetting. It is a better plan to welcome the puppy several days before or after the holiday week. Like a baby, your Dachshund puppy needs much rest and should not be over-handled. If not now, it soon will be "long enough for all the children to pet"; but in their first enthusiasm and rivalry, don't let them expedite the lengthening process by stretching the puppy. Once a child realizes that a puppy has "feelings" similar to his own, and can readily be hurt or injured, the opportunities for play and responsibilities provide exercise and training for both.

Lift a Dachshund either with one hand, by reaching across its back and placing your palm under its

Your New Dachshund Puppy

chest between its forelegs from behind, clasping its elbows with thumb and little finger; or with two hands, one under the chest and the other between the hind legs. The idea is to support the animal under the chest and the muscular thighs, which are firm enough to bear its weight. Children should use both hands to lift or carry even a small puppy. Hold the puppy securely, so that an unexpected wriggle or attempt to jump will not free it from your grasp and let it injure itself by falling; puppies have been known to break their necks!

Never lift a Dachshund by a pinch of skin on the neck or by its front feet or elbows; either of these actions could do permanent damage by stretching and loosening shoulder ligaments and elbow joints. For the same reason, a harness with a strap behind the elbows should never be worn by a Dachshund. And lifting under the soft belly may injure the internal organs.

Contrary to popular opinion, Dachshunds and cats can live happily together in the same household; and although the relationship is sooner established between puppies and kittens, a grown dog in most instances will benevolently accept a kitten, or a cat will be well-disposed toward a puppy. Mother cats have been known to wet-nurse very young Dachshund puppies. It is important, however, to place the cat's feeding dish on a shelf or table well out of reach of the Dachshund, or the more voracious dog will have consumed the cat's meal while the cat, with greater deliberation, is just beginning to think about eating. When dogs and cats are first brought together, keep them under observation to see if a friendly feeling develops; that one is not too strong or rough, even in play, for the other; that the cat has available high places for refuge. Some of our most amusing and rewarding experiences with animals have been due to the compatible companionship of Dachshunds and Persian, Siamese, and other cats which have shared their occasional fleas and our constant "bed and board" for thirty years.

First night—From its first arrival in your home, a Dachshund will spend half of its life sleeping. The first night that your puppy is put to bed without the company of other puppies, it may fret and whine. A carton inverted over its bed—with a door cut for access—may make the bed more cozy. If the crying keeps up, put the puppy back in bed, tuck it under its blanket (Dachshunds

Your New Dachshund Puppy

won't smother), and scold it to make repeated trips less and less attracitve to the puppy. If it still persists, try a loud whacking on the top of the box with a rolled newspaper. In a few days the carton can be left off. Some puppies seem to be comforted by the presence of a loud-ticking alarm clock in or near their bed. For company? Don't ask us why! Needless to say, the bed and newspaper should be accessible to each other.

A collar may be worn for an hour or two at a time to accustom the puppy to it. Choose a strong, buckled round collar, not less than "little-finger" thick; adjust it so that it cannot possibly pull off over the head. As the puppy grows up, its first collar may be outgrown. Never use a harness with a "belt" behind the elbows on a Dachshund puppy.

A leash may be snapped on and off the collar and the puppy allowed to get used to the feeling of these accessories. Then you can coax the puppy to follow you, by tone of voice, tidbits, and light persistent twitches on the leash; but don't drag a reluctant puppy. Starting to walk away often will persuade a puppy to follow, but don't drop the leash unless in a safely enclosed space.

Bed—The puppy should have a bed, located out of the way of

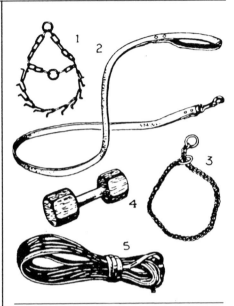

1. Limited choke collar. 2. Pliable leash, 6 feet long. 3. Chain choke collar. 4. Wooden dumbbell. 5. Long leash.

traffic, excitement, or drafts, where it can go of its own accord or on order; it should not be a place of penance but of relaxation and comfortable security. A basement is not a place suitable for continuous occupancy, and extensive separation from companionship may handicap development of desirable traits of disposition. Convenient to this bed, as explained under housebreaking, the puppy should have a newspaper pad which it can use as a bathroom whenever necessary, and know it will get praise for doing right, in the right place.

Your New Dachshund Puppy

A substantial corrugated carton will make a good temporary bed, which can be replaced if damaged, soiled, or outgrown. The front can be cut to a height over which the puppy can get in and out easily but will keep bedding in place and protect against drafts. Sides can slope up toward a higher back. Many puppies are used to torn newspapers as bedding.

When the puppy is first brought home, it can be carried to this bed, cuddled into a towel or blanket, petted, and the word "bed" repeated in fond tones until this sound is favorably associated by the puppy with this place. After that, when the puppy is near the bed, this word can be incorporated into a directive: "Come to your *bed*" if you are where you can tap it, or "Go to your *bed*" if you are a few steps away and can give a directional gesture with your hand. And of course, pet and praise the puppy when it arrives, continuing to repeat "bed" in endearing tones. Once a puppy learns this signal from nearby, it can be extended to increasing distances and become most useful.

When the puppy grows up and good habits are established, you may want to provide a furniture-type bed and a mattress pad. Cedar shavings, as a filler, discourage the presence of fleas. In winter, a quarter of an old wool blanket (in summer an old bath towel) is a good cover. Change and air this bedding frequently, and wash it when necessary.

Housebreaking—As this process may take some time, the new puppy should be quartered only in parts of the house where "mistakes" can. be cleaned up easily—on linoleum, tile, varnished or waxed floors, but no rugs or carpets. On a waterproof surface, put down an opened pad of newspapers to serve as a blotter. Recognition of this pad as the puppy's bathroom may be assured by bringing home, along with the puppy, a piece of paper already impregnated with its urine. Most puppies will prefer this paper pad to the more slippery floor; but they won't hit the center of the target every time, so leave plenty of waterproof border.

Young puppies empty their bladders frequently; playing *away* from the paper they don't at first anticipate the need of a trip *to* the paper. Keep newspapers in the bathroom, take the puppy when you go, open to doublepage size, and encourage the puppy to take an interest. As soon as it performs, it should be praised and released. If

Your New Dachshund Puppy

you use the same phrase, the puppy will come to associate it with elimination, and it becomes another useful signal. Started as praise "Used your *paper*" can be transformed into the command "Use your *paper*—or the word of your choice—provided that the operative word stays the same. Even if, from the start, you have a securely fenced yard, suitable for elimination, you still will need indoor facilities and means of segregation from rugs and carpets until bathroom habits become reliable; these facilities are also a great convenience in rugged weather or during your unexpectedly prolonged absence from home. And the "use your paper" drill saves time and worry if you ever take your dog visiting in private or public premises.

After each meal, the puppy should be confined to its newspapers, or put outdoors, as there is a peristaltic stimulation for elimination. It soon will learn to perform promptly to regain access to the companionship of the kitchen. As intervals between meals are increased, the puppy develops longer intervals between trips of necessity, and some happy day you will take note that it has been quite a while since an off-paper mistake. Then, when you know the puppy is "empty," it can have,

progressively, one, two, or three hours "out on parole" in other rooms of the house before again being confined to its linoleum quarters or put outdoors. Learning to anticipate is what takes time. Not until there is evidence that the puppy has become aware of impending elimination is there much use in remonstrating over mistakes. Never must a puppy be made to feel that elimination itself is wrong, only that there is a *right place* (by encouragement and praise) and later, when this is pretty well understood, that other places are wrong *as places* (by scolding the place, in the puppy's presence).

When you are sure that the puppy knows the geography of where it should go but makes an occasional mistake due to heedlessness or excitement, pick up the puppy (never call a puppy to you for disciplinary purposes), take it to the scene of the crime, scold it, and confine it until it has done right in the right place, before you praise and release it. Don't rub its nose in it; they know what it is without that. If the crime is repeated too often or if the culprit is caught in the act, a couple of punitive slaps on the plump little rump sometimes will help the impression sink in; and whatever you may hear, this will

Your New Dachshund Puppy

not make a puppy of sound temperament "hand shy." They associate too many favors with your hands for that. But never, except in emergency, strike a dog's face in discipline or fun.

Cleaning up—For mistakes on linoleum or tile, add a little chlorine bleach to wash water, or a little pine disinfectant for woodwork; pour through a rug or carpet, letting the spot dry over newspapers.

Time schedule—It is important to maintain the same daily routine— the time the family gets up and the puppy has its first outing, whether to paper, enclosed yard, or on leash; time of breakfast and next outing; time of any regular morning walk for exercise; time of family and puppy lunch, followed by another outing; time of any afternoon walk or other routine for an outing; time the puppy will be fed its supper with following outing; time of final snack and outing prior to bedtime. With such a regular schedule, a puppy will form correct habits in much less time than if there is no stabilized routine. And a regular schedule is particularly valuable in transferring a dog of any age from one place to another. This is notably useful in housebreaking a dog that has grown up in a kennel without such training, until free-

and-easy habits have become entrenched and harder to break.

On leash—The first few times you expect a puppy to eliminate while on collar and leash, it may take some extra time to overcome distractions. It will help if the "use your paper" type of signal has been previously impressed or if a piece of urine-scented paper is employed. Outdoor-trained puppies will be sure to perform promptly if the collar-and-leash project is added for a regular first-thing-in-the-morning or a last-thing-at-night trip. Never let a dog soil the sidewalk, and don't take your puppy into stores or other public buildings until you are sure that it will not embarrass you and discredit dog-owners generally.

Greeting efflux—A related problem is the dog, otherwise reliably housebroken, that loses control in the enthusiastic excitement of greetings. Such an animal is not aware of offending, and punishment only dampens the outpouring of its affections without overcoming the difficulty. Time usually corrects this habit. In the meantime, you can do something toward minimizing the inconvenience by selecting the greeting place, away from rugs or furniture, where cleaning-up is easy.

Grooming

Coats—When a Dachshund's skin and diet are right, it generates its own hair oil and rubbing or brushing brings the coat to a beautiful gloss. A smooth Dachshund coat requires no more care than to stroke it vigorously with the palm of your hand, or a "hound glove" if you prefer. Longhairs and wirehairs should be brushed daily to ensure that no dead hair accumulates. Burrs or tangles should be combed out as gently as you would treat your own hair; cut them out if need be rather than pull them out.

The growth rate of the coats of many *longhairs* is enough to compensate for the wear of regular work in punishing thicket and thorn. Such a coat grows in such bushy profusion that vigorous combing must replace the natural wear, or the dog's proper elegant outline and proportions are masked by "wool." Longer hair is specified as "fringe" or "frill" under neck and body, "feathers" on ears and behind legs, and "flag" under the tail. Excess hair should be removed from the elbows and from the feet where the standard refers to "mops" as "inelegant."

A proper close harsh wirehaired coat requires no special attention, except to remove untidy hairs, particularly on feet and elbows. Less harsh coats are sometimes improved by stripping the outer coat—and plucking, or with a stripping tool, but not clippers—and vigorous daily brushing during the couple of months it takes the new coat to grow in. Professional advice and instruction are desirable. Any scissors used around a dog should have blunt points.

Bathing a Dachshund regularly is not necessary or desirable. A dog's body temperature is not regulated by perspiration on the skin, but is "air-conditioned" by oral evaporation intensified by panting. Many a Dachshund has lived a long, happy and socially acceptable life without one bath. Bathing robs the skin of its natural hair oil. If a dog gets into something messy or smelly, use tepid water and a shampoo made especially for use on dogs; protect eyes and ears; lather and rinse twice until the coat is so soap-free that it "squeaks" when you rub it with your hand; towel briskly, and protect from drafts until thoroughly dry. Grooming the next day will restore natural gloss. When a Dachshund comes in from walking in wet or muddy weather, dry and clean him at the door, with a towel kept handy for that purpose.

Breed Standards

The standard of a breed is the criterion by which the appearance (and to a certain extent, the temperament) of any given dog is made subject, as far as possible, to objective measurement. Basically the standard for any breed is a definition of the perfect dog, to which all specimens of the breed are compared; the degree of excellence of the appearance of a given dog for conformation show purposes is in direct proportion to the dog's agreement with the requirements of the standard for its breed. Necessarily, of course, a certain amount of subjective evaluation is involved because of the wording of the standard itself and because of the factors introduced through the agency of the completely human judging apparatus. Breed standards are always subject to change through review by the national breed club for each dog, so it is always wise to keep up with developments in a breed by checking the publications of your national kennel club. (A list of the names and addresses of national kennel clubs for a number of English-speaking nations is included elsewhere in this book.) Although the standards of different national clubs are usually very much the same, there may be variances that must be noted if you plan to become seriously involved with breeding your dog or intend to show your dog on an international basis. For example, the Kennel Club of the United Kingdom allows separate championship status for all six varieties of Dachshund. The British standards also vary in respect to tail appearance and weight requirements. For the sake of brevity, only the official American standard for the Dachshund is included here in its entirety.

General Appearance: Low to ground, short-legged, long-bodied, but with compact figure and robust development; with bold and confident carriage of the head and intelligent facial expression. In spite of his shortness of leg, in comparison with his length of trunk, he should appear neither crippled, awkward, cramped in his capacity for movement, nor slim and weasel-like.

Qualities: He should be clever, lively, and courageous to the point of rashness, persevering in his work both above and below ground; with all the senses well developed. His build and disposition qualify him especially for hunting game below ground. Added to this, his hunting spirit, good nose, loud tongue, and

Breed Standards

small size, render him especially suited for beating the bush. His figure and his fine nose give him an especial advantage over most other breeds of sporting dogs for trailing.

Conformation of Body

Head: Viewed from above or from the side, it should taper uniformly to the tip of the nose, and should be clean-cut. The skull is only slightly arched, and should slope gradually without stop (the less stop the more typical) into the finely-formed slightly-arched muzzle (ram's nose). The bridge bones over the eyes should be strongly prominent. The nasal cartilage and tip of the nose are long and narrow; lips tightly stretched, well covering the lower jaw, but neither deep nor pointed; corner of the mouth not very marked. Nostrils well open. Jaws opening wide and hinged well back of the eyes, with strongly developed bones and teeth.

Teeth: Powerful canine teeth should fit closely together, and the outer side of the lower incisors should tightly touch the inner side of the upper. (Scissors bite.)

Eyes: Medium size, oval, situated at the sides, with a clean, energetic, though pleasant expression; not piercing. Color, lustrous dark reddish-brown to brownish-black for all coats and colors. Wall eyes in the case of dapple dogs are not a very bad fault,

but are also not desirable.

Ears: Should be set near the top of the head, and not too far forward, long but not too long, beautifully rounded, not narrow, pointed, or folded. Their carriage should be animated, and the forward edge should touch the cheek.

Neck: Fairly long, muscular, clean-cut, not showing any dewlap on the throat, slightly arched in the nape, extending in a graceful line into the shoulders, carried proudly but not stiffly.

Front: To endure the arduous exertion underground, the front must be correspondingly muscular, compact, deep, long and broad. Forequarters in detail:

Shoulder Blade: Long, broad, obliquely and firmly placed upon the fully developed thorax, furnished with hard and plastic muscles.

Upper Arm: Of the same length as the shoulder blade, and at right angles to the latter, strong of bone and hard of muscle, lying close to the ribs, capable of free movement.

Forearm: This is short in comparison to other breeds, slightly turned inwards; supplied with hard but plastic muscles on the front and outside, with tightly stretched tendons on the inside and at the back.

Joint between forearm and foot (wrists): These are closer together than the shoulder joints, so that the front

Breed Standards

does not appear absolutely straight.

Paws: Full, broad in front, and a trifle inclined outwards; compact, with well-arched toes and tough pads.

Toes: There are five of these, though only four are in use. They should be close together, with a pronounced arch; provided on top with strong nails, and underneath with tough toe-pads. Dewclaws may be removed.

Trunk: The whole trunk should in general be long and fully muscled. The back, with sloping shoulders, and short, rigid pelvis, should lie in the straightest possible line between the withers and the very slightly arched loins, these latter being short, rigid, and broad.

Chest: The breastbone should be strong, and so prominent in front that on either side a depression (dimple) appears. When viewed from the front, the thorax should appear oval, and should extend downward to the mid-point of the forearm. The enclosing structure of ribs should appear full and oval, and when viewed from above or from the side, full-volumed, so as to allow by its ample capacity, complete development of heart and lungs. Well ribbed up, and gradually merging into the line of the abdomen. If the length is correct, and also the anatomy of the shoulder and upper arm, the front leg when viewed in profile should cover the lowest point of the breast line.

Abdomen: Slightly drawn up.

Hindquarters: The hindquarters viewed from behind should be of completely equal width.

Croup: Long, round, full, robustly muscled, but plastic, only slightly sinking toward the tail.

Pelvic Bones: Not too short, rather strongly developed, and moderately sloping.

Thigh Bone: Robust and of good length, set at right angles to the pelvic bones.

Hind Legs: Robust and well-muscled, with well-rounded buttocks.

Knee Joint: Broad and strong.

Calf Bone: In comparison with other breeds, short; it should be perpendicular to the thigh bone, and firmly muscled.

The bones at the base of the foot (tarsus) should present a flat appearance, with a strongly prominent hock and a broad tendon of Achilles.

The central foot bones (metatarsus) should be long, movable toward the calf bone, slightly bent toward the front, but perpendicular (as viewed from behind).

Hind Paws: Four compactly closed and beautifully arched toes, as in the case of the front paws. The whole foot should be posed equally on the ball and not merely on the toes; nails short.

Tail: Set in continuation of the spine, extending without any pronounced curvature, and should not be carried too gaily.

Breed Standards

Note—Inasmuch as the Dachshund is a hunting dog, scars from honorable wounds shall not be considered a fault.

Special Characteristics of the Three Coat-Varieties

The Dachshund is bred with three varieties of coat: (1) Shorthaired (or *Smooth*); (2) Wirehaired; (3) Longhaired. All three varieties should conform to the characteristics already specified. The longhaired and shorthaired are old, well-fixed varieties, but into the wirehaired Dachshund, the blood of other breeds has been purposely introduced; nevertheless, in breeding him, the greatest stress must be placed upon conformity to the general Dachshund type. The following specifications are applicable separately to the three coat-varieties, respectively:

(1) Shorthaired (or Smooth) Dachshund

Hair: Short, thick, smooth and shining; no bald patches. Special faults are: Too fine or thin hair, leathery ears, bald patches, too coarse or too thick hair in general.

Tail: Gradually tapered to a point, well but not too richly haired, long, sleek bristles on the underside are considered a patch of strong-growing hair, not a fault. A brush tail is a fault, as is also a partly or wholly hairless tail.

Color of Hair, Nose and Nails:

One-Colored Dachshund: This group includes red (often called tan), red-yellow, yellow, and brindle, with or without a shading of interspersed black hairs. Nevertheless a clean color is preferable, and red is to be considered more desirable than red-yellow or yellow. Dogs strongly shaded with interspersed black hairs belong to this class, and not to the other color groups. A small white spot is admissible, but not desirable. Nose and Nails—Black; brown is admissible, but not desirable.

Two-Colored Dachshund: These comprise deep black, chocolate, gray (blue), and white; each with tan markings over the eyes, on the sides of the jaw and underlip, on the inner edge of the ear, front, breast, inside and behind the front legs, on the paws and around the anus, and from there to about one-third to one-half of the length of the tail on the under side. The most common two-colored Dachshund is usually called black-and-tan. A small white spot is admissible but not desirable. Absence, undue prominence or extreme lightness of tan markings is undesirable. Nose and Nails—In the

38

Breed Standards

case of black dogs, black; for chocolate, brown (the darker the better); for gray (blue) or white dogs, gray or even flesh color, but the last named color is not desirable; in the case of white dogs, black nose and nails are to be preferred.

Dappled Dachshund: The color of the dappled Dachshund is a clear brownish or grayish color, or even a white ground, with dark irregular patches of dark-gray, red-yellow or black (large areas of one color not desirable). It is desirable that neither the light nor the dark color should predominate. Nose and Nails—As for One- and Two-Colored Dachshund.

(2) Wirehaired Dachshund

The general appearance is the same as that of the shorthaired, but without being long in the legs, it is permissible for the body to be somewhat higher off the ground.

Hair: With the exception of jaw, eyebrows, and ears, the whole body is covered with perfectly uniform tight, short, thick, rough, hard coat, but with finer, shorter hairs (undercoat) everywhere distributed between the coarser hairs, resembling the coat of the German Wirehaired Pointer. There should be a beard on the chin. The eyebrows are bushy. On the ears the hair is shorter than on the body; almost

smooth, but in any case conforming to the rest of the coat. The general arrangement of the hair should be such that the wirehaired Dachshund, when seen from a distance should resemble the smooth-haired. Any sort of soft hair in the coat is faulty, whether short or long, or wherever found on the body; the same is true of long, curly, or wavy hair, or hair that sticks out irregularly in all directions; a flag tail is also objectionable.

Tail: Robust, as thickly haired as possible, gradually coming to a point, and without a tuft.

Color of Hair, Nose and Nails: All colors are admissible. White patches on the chest, though allowable, are not desirable.

(3) Longhaired Dachshund

The distinctive characteristic differentiating this coat from the short-haired, or smooth-haired Dachshund is alone the rather long silky hair.

Hair: The soft, sleek, glistening, often slightly wavy hair should be longer under the neck, on the underside of the body, and especially on the ears and behind the legs, becoming there a pronounced feather; the hair should attain its greatest length on the underside of the tail. The hair should fall beyond the lower edge of the ear. Short hair on the ear, so-called "leather" ears, is not desirable. Too

39

Breed Standards

luxurious a coat causes the longhaired Dachshund to seem coarse, and masks the type. The coat should remind one of the Irish Setter, and should give the dog an elegant appearance. Too thick hair on the paws, so-called "mops," is inelegant, and renders the animal unfit for use. It is faulty for the dog to have equally long hair over all the body, if the coat is too curly, or too scrubby, or if a flag or overhanging hair on the ears are lacking; or if there is a very pronounced parting on the back, or a vigorous growth between the toes.

Tail: Carried gracefully in prolongation of the spine; the hair attains here its greatest length and forms a veritable flag.

Color of Hair, Nose and Nails: Exactly as for the smooth-haired Dachshund, except that the red-with-black (heavily sabled) color is permissible and is formally classed as a red.

Miniature Dachshunds

Note—Miniature Dachshunds are bred in all three coats. Within the limits imposed, symmetrical adherence to the general Dachshund conformation, combined with smallness, and mental and physical vitality, should be the outstanding characteristics of Miniature Dachshunds. They have not been given separate classification but are a division of the Open Class for "under 10 pounds, and 12 months old or over."

General Faults

Serious Faults: Over- or undershot jaws, knuckling over, very loose shoulders.

Secondary Faults: A weak, long-legged, or dragging figure; body hanging between the shoulders; sluggish, clumsy, or waddling gait; toes turned inwards or too obliquely outwards; splayed paws; sunken back, roach (or carp) back; croup higher than withers; short-ribbed or too weak chest; excessively drawn-up flanks like those of a Greyhound; narrow, poorly-muscled hindquarters; weak loins; bad angulation in front or hindquarters; cowhocks; bowed legs; wall eyes, except for dappled dogs; bad coat.

Minor Faults: Ears wrongly set, sticking out, narrow or folded; too marked a stop; too pointed or weak a jaw; pincer teeth; too wide or too short a head; goggle eyes, wall eyes in the case of dappled dogs, insufficiently dark eyes in the case of all other coat-colors; dewlaps; short neck; swan neck; too fine or too thin hair; absence of, or too profuse or too light tan markings in the case of two-colored dogs.

Feeding

Now let's talk about feeding your dog, a subject so simple that it's amazing there is so much nonsense and misunderstanding about it. Is it expensive to feed a dog? No, it is not! You can feed your dog economically and keep him in perfect shape the year round, or you can feed him expensively. He'll thrive either way, and let's see why this is true.

First of all, remember a dog is a dog. Dogs do not have a high degree of selectivity in their food, and unless you spoil them with great variety (and possibly turn them into poor, "picky" eaters) they will eat almost anything that they become accustomed to. Many dogs flatly refuse to eat nice, fresh beef. They pick around it and eat everything else. But meat—bah! Why? They aren't accustomed to it! They are hounds. They'd eat rabbit fast enough, but they refuse beef because they aren't used to it.

Variety Not Necessary

A good general rule of thumb is forget all about human preferences and don't give a thought to variety. Choose the right diet for your dog and feed it to him day after day, year after year, winter and summer. But what is the right diet?

Hundreds of thousands of dollars have been spent in canine nutrition research. The results are pretty conclusive, so you needn't go into a lot of experimenting with trials of this and that every other week. Research has proven just what your dog needs to eat and to keep healthy.

Dog Food

There are almost as many right diets as there are dog experts, but the basic diet most often recommended is one that consists of a dry food, either meal or kibble form. There are several of these of excellent quality, manufactured by reliable concerns, research tested, and nationally advertised. They are inexpensive, highly satisfactory, and easily available in stores everywhere in containers of five to fifty pounds. Larger amounts cost less per pound, usually.

Feeding

If you have a choice of brands, it is usually safer to choose the better-known one; but even so, carefully read the analysis on the package. Do not choose any food in which the protein level is less than 25 percent, and be sure that this protein comes from both animal *and* vegetable sources. The good dog foods have meat meal, fish meal, liver, and such, plus protein from alfalfa and soybeans, as well as some dried-milk product. Note the vitamin content carefully. See that they are all there in good proportions; and be especially certain that the food contains properly high levels of vitamins A and D, two of the most perishable and important ones. Note the B-complex level, but don't worry about carbohydrate and mineral levels. These substances are plentiful and cheap and not likely to be lacking in a good brand.

The advice given for how to choose a dry food also applies to moist or canned types of dog foods, if you decide to feed one of these.

Having chosen a really good food, feed it to your dog as the manufacturer directs. And once you've started, stick to it. Never change if you can possibly help it. A switch from one meal or kibble-type food can usually be made without too much upset; however, a change will almost invariably give you (and the dog) some trouble.

Fat Important; Meat Optional

While the better dog foods are complete in themselves in every respect, there is one item to add to the food, and that is *fat*—any kind of melted animal fat. It can be lard, bacon, or ham fat or from beef, lamb, pork, or poultry. A grown dog should have at least a tablespoon or two of melted fat added to one feeding a day. If you feed your dog morning and night, give him half of the fat in each feeding.

The addition of meat to this basic ration is optional. There is a sufficient amount of everything your dog needs already in the food, but you may add any meat you wish, say, a half to a quarter of a pound. In adding meat, the glandular meats are best, such as kidneys, pork liver, and veal or beef heart. They are all cheap to buy and are far higher sources of protein than the usual muscle meat humans insist on. Cook these meats slightly or feed them raw. Liver and kidney should be cooked a little and fed sparingly since they are laxative to some dogs. Heart is ideal, raw or cooked. Or you can feed beef, lamb, ocean fish well cooked, and pork.

Feeding

When Supplements Are Needed

Now what about supplements of various kinds, mineral and vitamin, or the various oils? They are all okay to add to your dog's food. However, if you are feeding your dog a correct diet, and this is easy to do, no supplements are necessary unless your dog has been improperly fed, has been sick, or is having puppies. Vitamins and minerals are naturally present in all foods; and to ensure against any loss through processing, they are added in concentrated form to the dog food you use. Except on the advice of your veterinarian, extra and added amounts of vitamins can prove harmful to your dog! The same risk goes with minerals.

Feeding Schedule

When and how much food to give your dog? As to when (except in the instance of puppies which will be taken up later), suit yourself. You may feed two meals per day or the same amount in one single feeding, either morning or night. As to how to prepare the food and how much to give, it is generally best to follow the directions on the food package. Your own dog may want a little more or a little less.

Fresh, cool water should always be available to your dog. This is important to good health throughout his lifetime.

All Dogs Need to Chew

Puppies and young dogs need something with resistance to chew on while their teeth and jaws are developing—for cutting the puppy teeth, to induce growth of the permanent teeth under the puppy teeth, to assist in getting rid of the puppy teeth at the proper time, to help the permanent teeth through the gums, to ensure normal jaw development, and to settle the permanent teeth solidly in the jaws.

The adult dog's desire to chew stems from the instinct for tooth cleaning, gum massage, and jaw exercise—plus the need for an outlet for periodic doggie tensions.

This is why dogs, especially puppies and young dogs, will often destroy property worth hundreds of dollars when their chewing instinct is not diverted from their owner's possessions. And this is why you should provide your dog with something to chew—something that

Feeding

has the necessary functional qualities, is desirable from the dog's viewpoint, and is safe for your dog.

It is very important that dogs not be permitted to chew on anything they can break or on any indigestible thing from which they can bite sizeable chunks. Sharp pieces, such as from a bone which can be broken by a dog, may pierce the intestinal wall and kill. Indigestible things which can be bitten off in chunks, such as from shoes or rubber or plastic toys, may cause an intestinal stoppage (if not regurgitated) and bring painful death, unless surgery is promptly performed.

Strong natural bones, such as 4- to 8-inch lengths of round shin bone from mature beef—either the kind you can get from a butcher or one of the variety available commercially in pet stores—may serve your dog's teething needs if his mouth is large enough to handle them effectively. You may be tempted to give your puppy a smaller bone and he may not be able to break it when you do, but puppies grow rapidly and the power of their jaws constantly increases until maturity. This means that a growing dog may break one of the smaller bones at any time, swallow the pieces, and die painfully before you realize what is wrong.

All hard natural bones are highly abrasive. If your dog is an avid chewer, natural bones may wear away his teeth prematurely; hence, they then should be taken away from your dog when the teething purposes have been served. The badly worn, and usually painful, teeth of many mature dogs can be traced to excessive chewing on natural bones.

Contrary to popular belief, knuckle bones which can be chewed up and swallowed by the dog provide little, if any, useable calcium or other nutriment. They do, however, disturb the digestion of most dogs and cause them to vomit the nourishing food they need.

Dried rawhide products of various types, shapes, sizes, and prices are available on the market and have become quite popular. However, they don't serve the primary chewing functions very well; they are a bit messy when wet from mouthing, and most dogs chew them up rather rapidly—but they have been considered safe for dogs until recently. Now, more and more incidents of death, and near death, by strangulation have been reported to be the result of partially swallowed chunks of rawhide swelling in the throat. More

Feeding

recently, some veterinarians have been attributing cases of acute constipation to large pieces of incompletely digested rawhide in the intestine.

The nylon bones, especially those with natural meat and bone fractions added, are probably the most complete, safe, and economical answer to the chewing need. Dogs cannot break them or bite off sizeable chunks; hence, they are

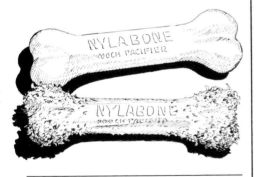

The upper Nylabone has not yet been chewed; the lower Nylabone shows normal signs of wear.

completely safe—and being longer lasting than other things offered for the purpose, they are economical.

Hard chewing raises little bristle-like projections on the surface of the nylon bones—to provide effective interim tooth cleaning and vigorous gum massage, much in the same way your toothbrush does it for you. The little projections are raked off and swallowed in the form of thin shavings, but the chemistry of the nylon is such that they break down in the stomach fluids and pass through without effect.

The toughness of the nylon provides the strong chewing resistance needed for important jaw exercise and effectively aids teething functions, but there is no tooth wear because nylon is non-abrasive. Being inert, nylon does not support the growth of microorganisms; and it can be washed in soap and water or it can be sterilized by boiling or in an autoclave.

Nylabone® is highly recommended by veterinarians as a safe, healthy nylon bone that can't splinter or chip. Nylabone® is frizzled by the dog's chewing action, creating a toothbrush-like surface that cleanses the teeth and massages the gums. Nylabone® and Nylaball® the only chew products made of flavor-impregnated solid nylon, are available in your local pet shop.

Nothing, however, substitutes for periodic professional attention to your dog's teeth and gums, not any more than your toothbrush can do that for you. Have your dog's teeth cleaned by your veterinarian at least once a year (twice a year is better) and he will be healthier, happier, and far more pleasant to live with.

Training

You owe proper training to your dog. The right and privilege of being trained is his birthright; and whether your dog is going to be a handsome, well-mannered housedog and companion, a show dog, or whatever possible use he may be put to, the basic training is always the same—all must start with basic obedience, or what might be called "manners training."

Your dog must come instantly when called and obey the "Sit" or "Down" command just as fast; he must walk quietly at "Heel," whether on or off the lead. He must be mannerly and polite wherever he goes; he must be polite to strangers on the street and in stores. He must be orderly in the presence of other dogs. He must not bark at children on roller skates, motorcycles, or domestic animals. And he must be restrained from chasing cats. It is not a dog's inalienable right to chase cats, and he must be reprimanded for it.

Professional Training

How do you go about this training? Well, it's a very simple procedure, pretty well standardized by now. First, if you can afford the extra expense, you may send your dog to a professional trainer, where in 30 to 60 days he will learn how to be a "good dog." If you enlist the services of a good professional trainer, follow his advice about when to come to see the dog. No, he won't forget you, but too-frequent visits at the wrong time may slow down his training progress. And using a "pro" trainer means you will have to go for some training, too, after the trainer feels your dog is ready to go home. You will have to learn how your dog works, just what to expect of him and how to use what the dog has learned after he is home.

Obedience Training Class

Another way to train your dog (many experienced dog people think this is the best) is to join an obedience-training class right in your own community. There is such a group in nearly every community nowadays. Here you will be working with a group of people who are also just starting out. You will actually be training your own dog, since all work is done under the direction of a head trainer who will make suggestions to you and also tell you when and how to correct your dog's errors. Then, too, working with

Training

such a group, your dog will learn to get along with other dogs. And, what is more important, he will learn to do exactly what he is told to do, no matter how much confusion there is around him or how great the temptation to go his own way.

Write to your national kennel club for the location of a training club or class in your locality. Sign up. Go to it regularly—every session! Go early and leave late! Both you and your dog will benefit tremendously.

Train Him By The Book

The third way of training your dog is by the book. Yes, you can do it this way and do a good job of it too. If you can read and if you're smarter than the dog, you'll do a good job. But in using the book method, select a book, buy it, study it carefully; then study it some more, until the procedures are almost second nature to you. *Then* start your training. But stay with the book and its advice and exercises. Don't start in and then make up a few rules of your own. If you don't follow the book, you'll get into jams you can't get out of by yourself. If after a few hours of short training sessions your dog is

still not working as he should, get back to the book for a study session, because it's *your* fault, not the dog's! The procedures of dog training have been so well systematized that it must be your fault, since literally thousands of fine dogs have been trained by the book.

After your dog is "letter perfect" under all conditions, then, if you wish, go on to advanced training and trick work.

Your dog will love his obedience training, and you'll burst with pride at the finished product! Your dog will enjoy life even more, and you'll enjoy your dog more. And remember—you *owe* good training to your dog!

There are a number of good books that give detailed training information.

Showing

A show dog is a comparatively rare thing. He is one out of several litters of puppies. He happens to be born with a degree of physical perfection that closely approximates the standard by which the breed is judged in the show ring. Such a dog should, at maturity, be able to win or approach his championship in good, fast company at the larger shows. Upon finishing his championship, he is apt to be highly desirable as a breeding animal. As a proven stud, he will automatically command a high price for service.

Showing dogs is a lot of fun—yes, but it is a highly competitive sport. Though all the experts were once beginners, the odds are against a novice. You will be showing against experienced handlers, both pro and amateur, people who have devoted a lifetime to breeding, picking the right ones, and then showing those dogs through to their championships. Moreover, the most perfect dog ever born has faults, and in your hands the faults will be far more evident than with the experienced handler who knows how to minimize his dog's faults. There are but a few points on the sad side of the picture.

The experienced handler, however, was not born knowing the ropes. He learned—*and so can you!* You can if you will put in the same time, study, and keen observation that he did. But it will take time!

Key to Success

First, search for a truly fine show-prospect puppy. Take the puppy home, raise him by the book, and, as carefully as you know how, give him every chance to mature into the dog hoped for. Some dog experts recommend keeping a show-prospect puppy out of big shows, even Puppy Classes, until he is mature. When he is approaching maturity, break him in at match shows (more on these later); after this experience for the dog and you, then go gunning for the big wins at the big shows.

Showing

must learn how to move properly at your side.

Enter Match Shows

Match shows differ from regular shows only in that no championship points are given. These shows are especially designed to launch young dogs (and young handlers) on a show career.

With the ring deportment you have watched at big shows firmly in mind and practice, enter your dog in as many match shows as you can. When in the ring, you have two jobs. One is to see to it that your dog is always being seen to best advantage. The other job is to keep your eye on the judge to see what he may want you to do next. Watch only the judge and your dog. Be quick and be alert; do exactly as the judge directs. Don't speak to him except to answer his questions. If he does something you don't like, don't say so. And don't irritate the judge (and everybody else) by constantly talking and fussing with your dog.

In moving about the ring, remember to keep clear of dogs beside you or in front of you. Many dog fanciers feel that you should *not* show your dog in a regular point show until he is at least close to maturity and after both you and he have had time to perfect ring manners and poise in the match shows.

Point Shows

Point shows are for purebred dogs registered with the club that is sanctioning the show. Each dog is entered in the show class which is appropriate for his age, sex, and previous show record. The show classes usually include Puppy, Novice, Bred-by-Exhibitor, American-bred, and Open; and there may also be a Veterans Class and Brace and Team Classes, among others.

There also may be a Junior Showmanship Class, a competition for youngsters. Young people between the ages of 10 and 16, inclusively, compete to see who best handles their dog, rather than to see which dog is best, as is done in the other classes.

For a complete discussion of show dogs, dog shows, and showing a dog, read *Successful Dog Show Exhibiting* by Anna Katherine Nicholas (T.F.H. Publications, Inc.).

Breeding

So you have a female dog and you want to breed her for a litter of puppies. Wonderful idea—very simple—lots of fun—make a lot of money. Well, it *is* a wonderful idea, but stop right there. It's not very simple—and you won't make a lot of money. Having a litter of puppies to bring up is

The external skeletal parts of a dog: 1. Cranium. 2. Cervical vertebra. 3. Thoracic vertebra. 4. Rib. 5. Lumber vertebra. 6. Ilium. 7. Femur. 8. Fibula. 9. Tibia. 10. Tarsus. 11. Metatarsus. 12. Phalanges. 13. Phalanges. 14. Ulna. 15. Radius. 16. Humerus. 17. Scapula.

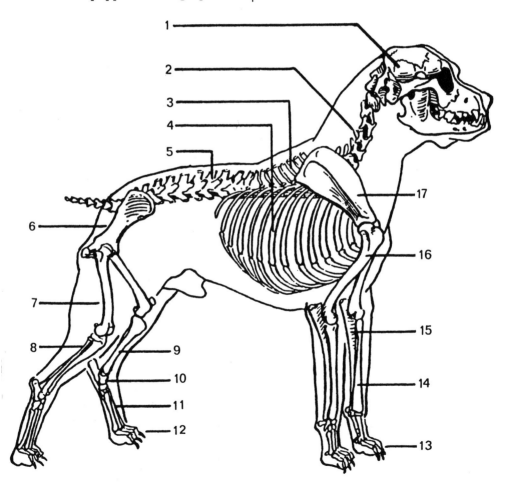

Breeding

hard, painstaking, thoughtful work; and only a few people regard such work as fun.

Breed Better Dogs

Bear in mind this very important point: Being a dog breeder is not just breeding dear Tillie to that darned good-looking male down the street. Would that it were that simple! Such a breeding will undoubtedly produce puppies. But that is not all you want. When you breed your female, it is only after the most careful planning—with every effort being made to be sure that the resulting puppies will be even better than the parent dogs (that they will come even closer to the standard than the parent animals) and that all the puppies will have good homes. Any fool can breed a litter of puppies; but only a careful, thoughtful, intelligent person can breed a litter of better puppies of your breed of dog. That must be your goal in breeding!

You can become a good novice breeder if you truly love the breed and are seriously concerned with the past, present, and future of the breed. You will breed your female only according to established scientific principles. Your personal sentiments have no place in the careful planning that goes on before you actually breed your female. The science of mammalian genetics is not a precise science like, say, mathematics. And the extensive reading you will do on the science (or art) of breeding dogs before you start to choose a stud will give you some idea of the variable factors you will be dealing with. It is a vast subject; but with the few brief pointers given here and additional reading and study, you can at least start on the right track.

Plan It on Paper

The principles of animal breeding are the same, whether the subjects be beef cattle, poultry, or dogs. To quote a cattle breeder, every breeding is first made "on paper" and later in the barnyard. In other words, first the blood strains of the animals are considered as to what goes well with what, so far as recorded ancestry is concerned. Having worked this out, the two animals to be mated must be studied and compared. If one does not excel where the other is lacking, at least in most points, then the paper planning must start over again and different animals be considered.

Breeding

With your own dog, there are several "musts" that are really axioms. First, breed only the best to the best. Two inferior animals will produce nothing but inferior animals, as surely as night follows day. To breed an inferior dog to another inferior one is a crime against the breed. So start by breeding the best to the best. And here again, an accurate knowledge of the standard is essential to know just what is best.

"Compensation" Breeding

No perfect dog has yet been whelped. Your female may be a winning show dog. She may be a champion. But she does have faults. In breeding her to a fine male, you must consider "compensation" breeding. She must compensate for his shortcomings and he for hers. For example, your female may be ideal in most respects but have faulty feet. So the male you choose, however ideal in other respects, *must* have ideal feet, as had his sire and dam too. In this way you may overcome the foot faults in your female's puppies.

This same principle applies to the correction of faults in any section of either male or female. But, you say, my dog has a pedigree as long as your arm. Must be good! Sad but true, a pedigree will not necessarily produce good puppies. A pedigree is no more—and no less—than your dog's recorded ancestry. Yes, you must know what dogs are in your dog's pedigree, but the most important point is, Were they good dogs? What were their faults and virtues? And to what degree did these dogs transmit these faults and virtues?

Breeding Methods

Now you may have heard that "like begets like." This is true and it is also false! Likes can beget likes only when both parent animals have the same likeness through generations of both family lines. The only way known to "fix" virtues and to eliminate faults is to mate two dogs of fairly close relationship bloodwise, two dogs which come from generations of likes and are family-related in their likeness. In this way you may ensure a higher and regular percentage of puppies which can be expected to mature into adults free at least from major faults under the standard. The likes must have the same genetic inheritance.

Through this "family" breeding, or line-breeding, correct type is set

Care of Mother and Family

and maintained. If both family lines are sound to begin with, family breeding and even close inbreeding (mating closely related dogs such as father and daughter) will merely improve the strain—but only in skilled hands. "Outcrossing" is mating dogs of completely different bloodlines with no, or only a few, common ancestors; it is used when undesirable traits begin to haunt closer breeding or when the breeder wants to bring in a specific trait or feature. The finest dogs today are the result of just such breeding methods. Study, expert advice, and experience will enable you, a novice, to follow these principles. So in your planning, forget the old nonsense about idiots and two-headed monsters coming from closely related parents.

Then, too, in your planning and reading, remember that intangible virtues, as well as physical ones, are without doubt inherited, as are faults in those intangibles. For example, in breeding bird dogs, where "nose sense" is of greatest importance, this factor can to a degree be fixed for future generations of puppies when the ancestors on both sides have the virtue of "nose sense." Just so, other characteristics of disposition or temperament can be fixed.

Let us assume that you have selected the right stud dog for your female and that she has been bred. In some 58 to 63 days, you will be presented with a nice litter of puppies. But there are a number of things to be gone over and prepared for in advance of the whelping date.

Before your female was bred, she was, of course, checked by your veterinarian and found to be in good condition and free from worms of any sort. She was in good weight but not fat. Once your female has been bred, you should keep your veterinarian informed of your female's progress; and when the whelping is imminent, your vet should be informed so that he can be on call in case any problems arise.

There's an old saying, "A litter should be fed from the day the bitch is bred," and there is a world of truth in it. So from the day your female is bred right up to the time the puppies are fully weaned, the mother's food is of the greatest importance. Puppies develop very rapidly in their 58 to 63 days of gestation, and their demands on the mother's system for nourishment are great. In effect, you are feeding your female and one to six or more other dogs, all at the same time.

Care of Mother and Family

The color captions for pages 57-64 can be found on page 16.

Additions to Regular Diet

For the first 21 days, your female will need but few additions to her regular diet. Feed her as usual, except for the addition of a small amount of "pot " or cottage cheese. This cheese, made from sour milk, is an ideal, natural source of added protein, calcium, and phosphorus—all essential to the proper growth of the unborn litter. Commercial vitamin-mineral supplements are unnecessary if the mother is fed the proper selection of natural foods.

Most commercial supplements are absolutely loaded with mineral calcium. You will usually find that the bulk of the contents is just plain calcium, a cheap and plentiful substance. Some dog experts believe, however, that calcium from an animal source like cheese is far more readily assimilated, and it is much cheaper besides. At any rate, do not use a commercial supplement without consulting your veterinarian and telling him the diet your dog is already getting.

Increase Food Intake

Along about the fifth week, the litter will begin to show a little, and now is the time to start an increase in food intake, not so much in bulk as in nutritive value. The protein content of your female's regular diet should be increased by the addition of milk products (cottage cheese, for example) meat (cooked pork liver, raw beef or veal heart, or some other meat high in protein), and eggs (either the raw yolk alone or, if the white is used, the egg should be cooked). Meanwhile, high-calorie foods should be decreased. The meat, cut into small pieces or ground, can be added to the basic ration. Mineral and vitamin supplements and cod-liver oil or additional fat also can be given to the female at this point, if your veterinarian so recommends.

Feed Several Times A Day

By now, your female is but a few weeks away from her whelping date, and the growing puppies are compressing her internal organs to an uncomfortable degree. She will have to relieve herself with greater frequency now. The stomach, too, is being compressed, so try reducing

Care of Mother and Family

the basic ration slightly and at the same time increasing the meats, eggs, and milk products. Feed several small meals per day in order to get in the proper, stepped-up quantity of food without causing the increased pressure of a single large meal. The bitch should be fed generously, but she should not be allowed to become overweight.

Regular Exercise Important

A great deal of advice has been given by experts on keeping the female quiet from the day she is bred all through the pregnancy. Such quiet, however, is not natural and it cannot be enforced. Naturally, the female should not be permitted to go in for fence jumping; but she will be as active as ever during the first few weeks and gradually she will, of her own accord, slow down appropriately, since no one knows quite as much about having puppies as the dog herself—up to a point. But see to it that your female has plenty of gentle exercise all along. She'll let you know when she wants to slow down.

The color captions for pages 57-64 can be found on page 16.

Treat her normally, and don't let her be the victim of all the sentimentality that humans with impending families are heir to.

Whelping Imminent

About the morning of the 58th day or shortly thereafter, your female, who now looks like an outsize beer barrel, will suddenly refuse her food. She may drink water, however. If you have been observant as things progressed, your hand, if not your eye, will tell you that the litter has dropped. The female now has a saggy abdomen, and this is the tip-off that whelping will occur soon, usually well within the next 24 hours. As the actual whelping hour approaches, the mother will become increasingly restless. She will seek out dark places like closets. She will scratch at the floor and wad up rugs as if making a bed. She is pretty miserable right now, so be gently sympathetic with her but *not maudlin!*

Get her to stay in the whelping box you have had prepared for several days. The floor of the box should be covered with an old blanket or towel so that she will feel comfortable there. When the whelping starts, replace the bedding

65

Care of Mother and Family

with newspapers; these can be replaced as they get scratched up or soiled.

The whelping box should be located in a warm, not hot, place free from drafts. The area should also be fairly quiet. You may, if you wish, confine her to the box by hitching her there with a leash to a hook three or four feet off the floor so she won't get twisted up in it. But when actual whelping starts, take off both leash and collar. Then, get yourself a chair and prepare for an all-night vigil. Somehow puppies always seem to be born at night, and the process is good for 12 to 14 hours usually.

Labor Begins

Stay with her when she starts to whelp, you and one other person she knows well and who is an experienced breeder. No audience, please! A supply of warm water, old turkish towels, and plenty of wiping rags are in order at this point.

When labor commences, the female usually assumes a squatting position, although some prefer to lie down. The first puppy won't look much like a puppy to you when it is fully expelled from the female. It will be wrapped in a dark, membranous sac, which the mother will tear open with her teeth, exposing one small, noisy pup—very wet. Let the mother lick the puppy off and help to dry it. She will also bite off the navel cord. This may make the puppy squeal, but don't worry, mama is not trying to eat her pup. The mother may eat a few of the sacs; this is normal. When she is through cleaning the puppy off, pick up the puppy and gently but firmly give it a good rubbing with a turkish towel. Do this in full sight of the mother and close enough so that she will not leave her whelping box.

When the puppy is good and dry and "squawking" a bit, place it near the mother or in a shallow paper box close to the mother so she can see it but will not step on it when she becomes restless with labor for the second puppy. If the room temperature is lower than 70 degrees, place a hot-water bottle wrapped in a towel near the puppies. Be sure to keep the water changed and warm so the puppies aren't lying on a cold water bottle. Constant warmth is essential.

Most dogs are easy whelpers, so you need not anticipate any trouble. Just stay with the mother, more as an observer than anything else. The experienced breeder who is keeping you company, or your vet, should handle any problems that arise.

66

Care of Mother and Family

Post-natal Care

When you are reasonably certain that the mother has finished whelping, have your veterinarian administer the proper amount of obstetrical pituitrin. This drug will induce labor again, thus helping to expel any retained afterbirth or dead puppy.

Inspect your puppies carefully. Rarely will any deformities be found; but if there should be any, make a firm decision to have your veterinarian destroy the puppy or puppies showing deformities.

During and after whelping, the female is very much dehydrated, so at frequent intervals she should be offered lukewarm milk or meat soup, slightly thickened with well-soaked regular ration. She will relish liquids and soft foods for about 24 hours, after which she will go back to her regular diet. But be sure she has a constant supply of fresh water available. Feed her and keep her water container outside the whelping box.

After all of the puppies have been born, the mother might like to go outside for a walk. Allow her this exercise. She probably won't want to be away from her puppies more than a minute or two.

The puppies will be blind for about two weeks, with the eyes gradually opening up at that time.

The little pups will be quite active and crawl about over a large area. Be sure that all of the puppies are getting enough to eat. If the mother sits or stands, instead of lying still to nurse, the probable cause is scratching from the puppies nails. You can remedy this by clipping them, as you do hers.

Weaning Time

Puppies can usually be completely weaned at six weeks of age, although you can start to feed them at three weeks. They will find it easier to lap semi-solid food. At four weeks they should be given four meals a day, and soon they will do without their mother entirely. Start them on mixed dog food, or leave it with them in a dish for self-feeding. Don't leave water with them all the time; at this age everything is to play with and they will use it as a wading pool. They can drink all they need if it is offered several times a day, after meals.

As the puppies grow up, the mother will go into the box only to nurse them, first sitting up and then standing. The periods of time between the mother's visits to the box will gradually lengthen, until it is no longer necessary for her to nurse the pups.

Health and Disease

First, don't be frightened by the number of health problems that a dog might have over the course of his life-time. The majority of dogs never have any of them. Don't become a dog-hypochondriac. All dogs have days when they feel lazy and want to lie around doing nothing. For the few problems that you might be concerned about, remember that your veterinarian is your dog's best friend. When you first get your puppy, select a veterinarian whom you have faith in. He will get to know your dog and will be glad to have you consult him for advice. A dog needs little medical care, but that little is essential to his good health and well-being. He needs a proper diet given at regular hours; clean, roomy housing; daily exercise; companionship and love; frequent grooming; and regular check-ups by your veterinarian.

Using a Thermometer and Giving Medicines

Almost every serious ailment shows itself by an increase in the dog's body temperature. If your dog acts lifeless, looks dull-eyed, and gives the impression of illness,

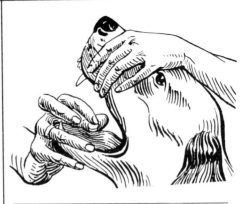

The proper way to give a pill or tablet.

check his temperature by using a rectal thermometer made of either plastic or glass. Hold the dog securely, insert the thermometer (which you have lubricated with petroleum jelly), and take a reading. The average normal temperature for your dog will be 101.5 °F. Excitement may raise the temperature slightly; but any rise of

The proper way to give liquid medication.

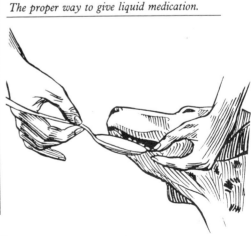

Health and Disease

more than a few points is cause for alarm, and your vet should be consulted.

Giving medicines to your dog is not really difficult. In order to administer a liquid medication, do not open the dog's mouth. Instead, form a pocket by pulling out the lower lip at the corner of the mouth; pour the medicine in with a spoon; hold the head only very slightly upward. (If the head is held too high, the medicine may enter the windpipe instead of the passage to the stomach, thus choking the dog.) With agitated animals, medicine can still be given by this method, even though the dog's mouth is held shut with a tape or a muzzle.

In order to administer a pill or tablet, raise your dog's head slightly and open his mouth. (Using one hand, grasp the cheeks of the dog, and then press inward. The pressure of the lips pushed against the teeth will keep the mouth open). With the other hand, place the pill or tablet far back on the middle of the tongue. Quickly remove your hand from the dog's cheeks; hold the dog's mouth closed (but not too tightly), and gently massage his throat. You can tell the medicine has been swallowed when the tip of the dog's tongue shows between his front teeth.

A Vaccination Schedule

Prevention is the key word for many dog diseases, and the best prevention is a series of vaccinations administered by your veterinarian. Such contagious diseases as distemper, hepatitis, parainfluenza, leptospirosis, rabies, and canine parvovirus can be virtually eliminated by strictly following a vaccination schedule.

Distemper is probably the most virulent of all dog diseases. Young dogs are most susceptible to it, although it may affect dogs of all ages. The dog will lose his appetite, seem depressed, feel chilled, and run a fever. Often he will have a watery discharge from his eyes and nose. Unless treated promptly, the disease goes into advanced stages with infections of the lungs, intestines, and nervous system; and dogs that recover may be left with some impairment such as paralysis, convulsions, a twitch, or some other defect, usually spastic in nature. The best protection against this is very early inoculation with a series of permanent shots and a booster shot each year thereafter.

Hepatitis is a viral disease spread by contact. The initial symptoms of drowsiness, vomiting, great thirst, loss of appetite, and a high temperature closely resemble those

Health and Disease

of distemper. These symptoms are often accompanied by swellings of the head, neck, and abdomen. The disease strikes quickly; death may occur in just a few hours. Protection is afforded by injection with a vaccine.

Parainfluenza is commonly called "kennel cough." Its main symptom is coughing; and since it is highly contagious, it can sweep through an entire kennel in just a short period of time. A vaccination is a dog's best protection against this respiratory disease.

Leptospirosis is caused by bacteria that live in stagnant or slow-moving water. It is carried by rats and mice, and infection is begun by the dog licking substances contaminated by the urine or feces of infected animals. The symptoms are diarrhea and a yellowish-brownish discoloration of the jaws, tongue, and teeth, caused by an inflammation of the kidneys. This disease can be cured if caught in time, but it is best to ward it off with a vaccine which your veterinarian can administer.

Rabies is an acute disease of the dog's central nervous system. It is spread by infectious saliva transmitted by the bite of an infected animal. Rabies is generally manifested in one or the other of two groups of symptoms, and the

symptoms usually appear within five days. The first is "furious rabies," in which the dog exhibits changes in his personality. The dog becomes hypersensitive and runs at and bites everything in sight. Eventually, the animal's lower jaw becomes paralyzed and hangs down; he walks with a stagger and saliva drips from his mouth. The second syndrome is referred to as "dumb rabies" and is characterized by the dog's walking in a bearlike manner, head down. The lower jaw is paralyzed, and the dog is unable to bite. Outwardly, it may seem as though he has a bone caught in his throat.

Even if your pet should be bitten by a rabid dog or other animal, he probably can be saved if you get him to the veterinarian in time for a series of injections. However, after the symptoms have appeared, no cure is possible. Remember that an annual rabies inoculation is almost certain protection against rabies. If you suspect that your dog or some other animal has rabies, notify your local health department. A rabid animal is a danger to all who come near him.

Canine parvovirus is a highly contagious viral disease that attacks the intestinal tract, white blood cells, and less frequently the heart muscle. It is believed to spread through dog-to-dog contact (the specific source of infection being the fecal matter of infected dogs), but it can also be transmitted from place to place on the hair and feet of infected dogs and by contact with contaminated cages, shoes, and the like. It is particularly hard to overcome because it is capable of existing in the environment for many months under varying conditions, unless strong disinfectants are used.

The symptoms are vomiting, fever, diarrhea (often blood-streaked), depression, loss of appetite, and dehydration. Death may occur in only two days. Puppies are hardest hit, with the virus being fatal to 75 percent of the puppies that contact it. Older dogs fare better; the disease is fatal to only two to three percent of those afflicted.

The best preventive measure for parvovirus is vaccination administered by your veterinarian. Precautionary measures individual pet owners can take include disinfecting the kennel and other areas where the dog is housed. One part sodium hypochlorite solution (household bleach) to 30 parts of water will do the job efficiently. Keep the dog from coming into contact with the fecal matter of other dogs when walking or exercising your pet.

Internal Parasites

There are four common internal parasites that may infect your dog. These are roundworms, hookworms, whipworms, and tapeworms. The first three can be diagnosed by laboratory examination; the presence of tapeworms is determined by seeing segments in the stool or attached to the hair around the tail. Do not under any circumstances attempt to worm your dog without the advice of your veterinarian. After first determining what type of worm or worms are present, he will advise you of the best method of treatment.

A dog or puppy in good physical condition is less susceptible to worm infestation than a weak dog. Proper sanitation and a nutritious diet help in preventing worms. One of the best preventive measures is to always have clean, dry bedding for

Adult whipworms are between two and three inches long, and the body of each worm is no thicker than a heavy sewing needle.

71

your dog. This will diminish the possibility of reinfection due to flea or tick bites.

Heartworm infestation in dogs is passed by mosquitoes and can be a life-threatening problem. Dogs with the disease tire easily, have difficulty breathing, cough, and may lose weight despite a hearty appetite. If caught in the early stages, the disease can be effectively treated; however, the administration of daily preventive medicine throughout the spring, summer, and fall months is strongly advised. Your veterinarian must first take a blood sample from your dog to test for the presence of the disease. If the dog is heartworm-free, pills or liquid medicine can be prescribed that will protect against any infestation.

Above: Red mange mite.

Below: The common dog flea.

A female dog tick that is gorged with blood.

Below: The under side of a sarcoptic mange mite.

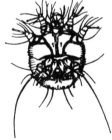

Health and Disease

External Parasites

Fleas and ticks are the two most common external parasites that can trouble a dog. Along with the general discomfort and irritation that they bring to a dog, these parasites can infest him with worms and disease. The flea is a carrier of tapeworm and may act as an intermediate host for heartworm. The tick can cause dermatitis and anemia, and it may also be a carrier of Rocky Mountain spotted fever and canine babesiasis, a blood infection. If your dog becomes infested with fleas, he should be treated with a medicated dip bath or some other medication recommended by your vet. Ticks should be removed with great care;

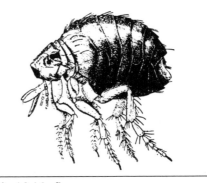

A sticktight flea.

you must be certain that the head of the tick is not left in the dog—this could be a source of infection.

Two types of mange, sarcoptic and follicular, are also caused by parasites. The former is by far the more common and results in an intense irritation, causing violent scratching. Close examination will reveal small red spots which become filled with pus. This is a highly

A female tick.

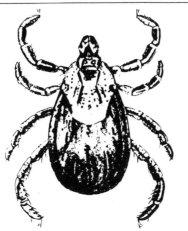

A male tick.

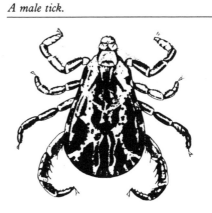

Health and Disease

contagious condition, and any dog showing signs of the disease should be isolated. Consult your veterinarian for the proper treatment procedures. Follicular mange is very much harder to cure; but fortunately, it is much rarer and less contagious. This disease will manifest itself as bare patches appearing in the skin, which becomes thickened and leathery. A complete cure from this condition is only rarely effected.

Other Health Problems

Hip dysplasia is an often crippling condition more prevalent in large

A dislocation of the upper leg bone. Dislocations should be immediately attended to by your vet.

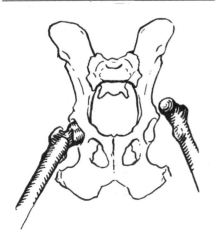

breeds than in small, but it has occurred in almost every breed. The cause is not known absolutely, though it is believed to be hereditary, and as yet there is no known cure. The condition exists in varying degrees of severity. In general, hip dysplasia can be described as a poor fit between the two bones of the hip joint and is caused by a malformation of one or the other. The condition causes stiffness in the hindlegs, considerable pain in the more severe cases, and difficulty of movement. It generally manifests itself in puppyhood and can be noticed by the time the young dog is two months old. If hip dysplasia is suspected, the dog should be x-rayed; and if afflicted, it should not be used for breeding. When the pain is severe and continual, euthanasia is occasionally recommended, though medication is available to control the pain and allow the dog to move with more ease.

Coughs, colds, bronchitis, and pneumonia are respiratory diseases that may affect the dog. Being subjected to cold or a draft after a bath, sleeping near an air conditioner or in the path of a fan, or resting near a radiator can cause respiratory ailments. The symptoms are similar to those in humans;

however, the germs of these diseases are different and do not affect both dogs and humans, so they cannot be infected by each other. Treatment is much the same as for a child with the same type of illness. Keep the dog warm, quiet, and well fed. Your veterinarian has antibiotics and other remedies to help the dog recover.

Eczema is a disease that occurs most often in the summer months and affects the dog down the back, especially just above the root of the tail. It should not be confused with mange, as it is not caused by a parasite. One of the principle causes of eczema is improper nutrition, which makes the dog susceptible to disease. Hot, humid weather promotes the growth of bacteria, which can invade a susceptible dog and thereby cause skin irritation and lesions. It is imperative that the dog gets relief from the itching that is symptomatic of the disease, as self-mutilation by scratching will only help to spread the inflammation. Antibiotics may be necessary if a bacterial infection is, indeed, present.

Moist eczema, commonly referred to as "hot spots," is a rapidly appearing skin disease that produces a moist infection. Spots appear very suddenly and may spread rapidly in a few hours, infecting several parts of the body. These lesions are generally bacterially infected and are extremely itchy, which will cause the dog to scratch frantically and further damage the afflicted areas. Vomiting, fever, and an enlargement of the lymph nodes may occur. The infected areas must be clipped to the skin and thoroughly cleaned. Your veterinarian will prescribe an anti-inflammatory drug and antibiotics, as well as a soothing emollient to relieve itching.

The *eyes*, because of their sensitivity, are prone to injury and infection. Dogs that spend a great deal of time outdoors in heavily wooded areas may return from an exercise excursion with watery eyes, the result of brambles and high weeds scratching them. The eyes may also be irritated by dirt and other foreign matter. Should your dog's eyes appear red and watery, a mild solution can be mixed at home for a soothing washing. Your veterinarian will be able to tell you what percentage of boric acid, salt, or other medicinal compound to mix with water. You must monitor your dog's eyes after such a solution is administered; if the irritation persists, or if there is a significant discharge, immediate veterinary attention is warranted.

Your dog's *ears*, like his eyes, are extremely sensitive and can also be

Health and Disease

prone to infection, should wax and/or dirt be allowed to build up. Ear irritants may be present in the form of mites, soap or water, or foreign particles which the dog has come into contact with while romping through a wooded area. If your dog's ears are bothering him, you will know it—he will scratch his ears and shake his head, and the ears will have a foul-smelling dark secretion. This pasty secretion usually signals the onset of *otorrhea*, or ear canker, and at this stage proper veterinary care is essential if the dog's hearing is not to be permanently impaired. In the advanced stages of ear canker, tissue builds up within the ear, and the ear canal becomes blocked off, thus diminishing the hearing abilities of that ear. If this is to be prevented, you should wash your dog's ears, as they require it, with a very dilute solution of hydrogen peroxide and water, or an antibacterial ointment, as your vet suggests. In any case,

An ear mite.

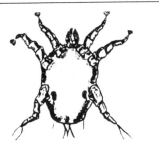

the ears, because of their delicacy, are to be washed gently, with a soft cloth or cotton.

Your pet's *teeth* can be maintained by his regular use of a chew product such as Nylabone® or Nylaball,® which serves to clean the teeth of tartar accumulation and to massage and stimulate the gums. Tartar accumulates on the teeth of dogs, particularly at the gum line, more rapidly than on the teeth of humans; and these accumulations, if not removed, bring irritation, infection and, ultimately, destruction of the teeth at the roots. With puppies, a chew product helps to relieve the discomfort of the teething stage and, of course, prevents the pup's chewing of your furniture and slippers! A periodic inspection of your dog's mouth will alert you to any problem he might have which would require a trip to the veterinarian's office. Any signs of tooth or gum sensitivity, redness, or swelling, signal the need for professional treatment.

A dog's *nails* should not be allowed to become overlong. If you live in a city and walk your dog regularly on pavement, chances are that his nails are kept trimmed from the "wear and tear" they receive from the sidewalks. However, if your dog gets all of his exercise in your yard, or if his nails simply

Health and Disease

grow rather quickly, it will occasionally be necessary for you to clip his nails. It is best for you to have your veterinarian show you the proper way to perform the nail clipping. Special care must always be taken to avoid cutting too far and reaching the "quick." If you cut into the quick of the nail, it will bleed, so it is easy to see why an expert must show you the proper procedure. A nail clipper designed especially for dogs can be purchased at any pet shop.

Emergency First Aid

If you fear that your dog has swallowed *poison*, immediately get him to the veterinarian's. Try to locate the source of poisoning; if he has swallowed, for example, a cleaning fluid kept in your house, check the bottle label to see if inducing the dog to vomit is necessary. Inducing the dog to vomit can be very harmful, depending upon the type of poison swallowed. Amateur diagnosis is very dangerous.

Accidents, unfortunately, do happen, so it is best to be prepared. If your dog gets hit by a car or has a bad fall, keep him absolutely quiet, move him as little as possible, and get veterinary treatment as soon as possible. It is unwise to give any stimulants such as brandy or other alcoholic liquids when there is visible external hemorrhage or the possibility of internal hemorrhaging.

Minor cuts and wounds will be licked by your dog, but you should treat such injuries as you would your own. Wash out the dirt and apply an antiseptic.

Severe cuts and wounds should be bandaged as tightly as possible to stop the bleeding. A wad of cotton may serve as a pressure bandage, which will ordinarily stop the flow of blood. Gauze wrapped around the cotton will hold it in place. Usually applying such pressure to a wound will sufficiently stop the blood flow; however, for severe bleeding, such as when an artery is cut, a tourniquet may be necessary. Apply a tourniquet between the injury and the heart if the bleeding is severe. To tighten the tourniquet, push a pencil through the bandage and twist it. Take your dog to a veterinarian immediately, since a tourniquet should not be left in place any longer than fifteen minutes.

Minor burns or scalds can be treated by clipping hair away from the affected area and then applying a paste of bicarbonate of soda and water. Apply it thickly to the burned area and try to keep the dog

Care of the Oldster

from licking it off.

Serious burns require the immediate attention of your veterinarian, as shock quickly follows such a burn. The dog should be kept quiet, wrapped in a blanket; and if he still shows signs of being chilled, use a hot-water bottle. Clean the burn gently, removing any foreign matter such as bits of lint, hair, grass, or dirt; and apply cold compresses. Act as quickly as possible. Prevent exposure to air by covering with gauze, cotton, and a loose bandage. To prevent the dog from interfering with the dressing, muzzle him and have someone stay with him until veterinary treatment is at hand.

Stings from wasps and bees are a hazard for the many dogs that enjoy trying to catch these insects. A sting frequently follows a successful catch, and it often occurs inside the mouth, which can be very serious. The best remedy is to get him to a veterinarian as soon as possible, but there are some precautionary measures to follow in the meantime. If the dog has been lucky enough to be stung only on the outside of the face, try to extricate the stinger; then swab the point of entry with a solution of bicarbonate of soda. In the case of a wasp sting, use vinegar or some other acidic food.

Barring accident or disease, your dog is apt to enjoy a life of 12 to 14 years. However, beginning roughly with the eighth year, there will be a gradual slowing down. And with this there are many problems of maintaining reasonably good health and comfort for all concerned.

While there is little or nothing that can be done in the instance of failing sight and hearing, proper management of the dog can minimize these losses. Fairly close and carefully supervised confinement are necessary in both cases. A blind dog, otherwise perfectly healthy and happy, can continue to be happy if he is always on a leash outdoors and guided so that he does not bump into things. Indoors, he will do well enough on his own. Dogs that are sightless seem to move around the house by their own radar system. They learn where objects are located; but once they do learn the pattern, care must be taken not to leave a piece of furniture out of its usual place.

Deafness again requires considerable confinement, especially in regard to motor traffic and similar hazards; but deafness curtails the dog's activities much less than blindness. It is not necessary to send any dog to the Great Beyond

Care of the Oldster

because it is blind or deaf—if it is otherwise healthy and seems to enjoy life.

Teeth in the aging dog should be watched carefully, not only for the pain they may cause the dog but also because they may poison the system without any local infection or pain. So watch carefully, especially when an old dog is eating. Any departure from his usual manner should make the teeth suspect at once. Have your veterinarian check the teeth frequently.

His System Slows Down

As the dog ages and slows down in his physical activity, so his whole system slows down. With the change, physical functions are in some instances slowed and in others accelerated—in effect, at least.

For example, constipation may occur; and bowel movements may become difficult, infrequent, or even painful. Chronic constipation is a problem for your veterinarian to deal with; but unless it is chronic, it is easily dealt with by adding a little extra melted fat to the regular food. Do not increase roughage or administer physics unless so directed by your veterinarian. If the added

fat in the food doesn't seem to be the answer to occasional constipation, give your dog a half or a full teaspoon of mineral oil two or three times a week. Otherwise, call your veterinarian.

On either side of the rectal opening just below the base of the tail are located the two anal glands. Occasionally these glands do not function properly and may cause the dog great discomfort if not cleaned out. This is a job for your veterinarian, until after he has shown you how to do it.

Watch His Weight

In feeding the aging dog, try to keep his weight down. He may want just as much to eat as ever, but with

An easy way to weigh your dog is to hold the dog while you stand on a scale, and then subtract your weight from the total.

Care of the Oldster

decreased activity he will tend to put on weight. This weight will tend to slow down all other bodily functions and place an added strain on the heart. So feed the same diet as usual, but watch the weight.

Age, with its relaxing of the muscles, frequently makes an otherwise clean dog begin to misbehave in the house, particularly so far as urination is concerned. There is little that can be done about it, if your veterinarian finds there is no infection present, except to give your dog more frequent chances to urinate and move his bowels. It's just a little bit more work on your part to keep your old friend more comfortable and a "good" dog.

Let your dog exercise as much as he wants to without encouraging him in any violent play. If he is especially sluggish, take him for a walk on a leash in the early morning or late evening. Avoid exercise for him during the heat of the day. And in cold weather or rain, try a sweater on him when he goes out. It's not "sissy" to put a coat on an old dog. You and your veterinarian, working closely together, can give your dog added life and comfort. So consult your veterinarian often.

Occasionally in an old dog there is a problem of unpleasant smell, both bodily and orally. If this situation is acute, it is all but unbearable to have the dog around. But the situation can be corrected or at least alleviated with frequent and rather heavy dosing of chlorophyll. A good rubdown with one of the dry-shampoo products is also helpful.

When the End Comes

People who have dogs are sooner or later faced with the tragedy of losing them. It's tough business losing a dog, no matter how many you may have at one time. And one dog never takes the place of another—so don't expect it to. When you lose your dog, get another as quickly as you can. It does help a lot.

Keep your dog alive as long as he is happy and comfortable. Do everything you reasonably can to keep him that way. But when the sad time comes that he is sick, always uncomfortable, or in some pain, it is your obligation then to have him put away. It is a tough ordeal to go through, but you owe it to your old friend to allow him to go to sleep. And, literally, that's just what he does. Your veterinarian knows what to do. And your good old dog, without pain, fright, bad taste, or bad smells, will just drift to sleep.